Assessments and Lesson Plans

for

Graves, Juel, and Graves

Teaching Reading in the 21ˢᵗ Century

Fourth Edition

prepared by

Robert C. Calfee
University of California, Riverside

Kathleen M. Wilson
University of Nebraska, Lincoln

Michael F. Graves
University of Minnesota

PEARSON

Boston   New York   San Francisco
Mexico City   Montreal   Toronto   London   Madrid   Munich   Paris
Hong Kong   Singapore   Tokyo   Cape Town   Sydney

Table of Contents

Part One: Assessments

Part Two: Lesson Plans

Tile Test

Grade Level: Kindergarten – 2nd Grade

The Tile Test is designed to quickly assess students' understanding of letters, sounds, words, and sentences. Meta-linguistic questions encourage students to talk about the strategies they use when decoding and spelling words.

General Procedures

1. Start with a collection of letter tiles, not just one card.
2. Allow sufficient time for each response.
3. Provide general positive feedback to encourage students, do not correct mistakes.
4. Write the students' responses to each item:
    a. Correct response is marked + or ✓,
    b. Incorrect responses will be recorded in full,
    c. No response will be recorded as dk (Doesn't Know),
    d. Self Correction is marked SC and counted as correct.
    e. Segmented words read without blending sounds will be marked with slashes between sounds e.g. /t/a/p/.
5. Administer all components.
6. Stop Rule, if a student is unable to respond to any word of the first 4 items use teacher judgment to discontinue this segment and move to the next. If a student is unsuccessful in reading the word tiles at all do not proceed o sentence reading.

Letters and Sounds

Begin with a collection of letter tiles [**m, a, p, i, f, s, t, d, n**].
1. Have students point to the letter you name.
2. Ask students to tell you the <u>name</u> and <u>sound</u> of each letter.

Words

Add the following letters to the collection of letter tiles [h, e, w, c, k, v, u, l, s, o, d, d, b, r, p, g].
1. Manipulate individual letters to build the given words. The teacher builds, and the student reads. Follow-up with the Articulation and Metalinguistic (ML) questions below.
2. Ask the student to use the letter tiles to build the words you read. (Articulation and ML) Record student responses. Observe and record strategy use (i.e., orally articulating sounds) and behaviors.
3. Use the word tiles provided on a separate sheet to assess word reading, Leave word tiles on the table for use in the next section.

<u>**Metalinguistic (ML) and Articulation Questions:**</u> Following the reading of 'pat' and 'sat' and the building of 'tan' and 'tad,' ask how the student knew to make the change(s) he or she made. After the successful reading or building of their most difficult word, ask the

student what his or her mouth did to say the first sound of the word. Then ask how he or she knew to read / build the word that way? Record student responses. Provide and document probing questions as necessary. (Examples: What were you looking at? I noticed your mouth moving, how did that help you?) Score the ML questions using the Tile Test Meta-language Rubric.

Sentences

Use the collection of words to create sentences. Record student responses.
1. Using the word cards, build each sentence and have the student read.
2. Ask the student to use the word cards to build sentences you read. Then ask the student to read the sentence they built. Record student responses.
3. Hand the student the sentence on the separate sheet and have the student read it. Record student responses.

TILE TEST META-LANGUAGE RUBRIC

0	No Response; "I don't know"
1	"I know it." "My mom taught me." "I'm smart."
2	Recognition of letters; "I looked at the letters."
3	Recognition of sounds; "I sound it out." "I listen to the sounds."
4	Partial linking sounds to letters; "It starts with a P /p/, then /□/ " Or Partial analogy "Pat is like cat"
5	Explains spelling of <u>each</u> sound. Or full analogy "Pat is like cat, but it starts with a /p/."
6	Explains how sounds are articulated. "It starts with /p/ my lips are together and the air pops out, my tongue is resting in the middle of my mouth…".

Tile Test: Recording Sheet

Student _____Date _____School_____Teacher_____

Letter Identification: Lay out letter tiles [**m, a, p, i, f, s, t, d, n**].
"Here are some letters. I'll say the name of a letter and ask you to point to the letter. Point to the card that has the letter m." (*Record, continue procedure*)
"Now, I'll point to a card and you'll tell me two things about the letter. First, the <u>name</u> of the letter, and second, the <u>sound</u> that it makes." (*Record*)

	Identification	Name	Sound			Identification	Name	Sound
m	_____				s	_____		
a	_____				t	_____		
p	_____				d	_____		
i	_____				n	_____		

Words:
Add these letter tiles to the tiles above: [**b, c, d, d, e, h, k, l, o, r, r, s, u, v, w**].
"Now let's put some letters together to make words. Some of the words are real words and some are pretend words. I'll go first and make a word, and then I'll ask you to read it for me." (*Manipulate only necessary letters, stop after sat and ask the first ML & articulation questions.*)

↓pat	_____		vute	_____
*sat	_____		flass	_____
sam	_____		lodded	_____
hin	_____		wembick	_____

*ML: "I noticed that you said 'sat' (*or repeat what the student said if different*). How did you know to change it that way from 'pat' (*or repeat what the student said*)?"_____
_____
_____

Articulation: "Tell me what your mouth did to say the first sound in _____ ." (*Repeat the most difficult word they read correctly.*) Record verbal responses and behaviors.
_____
_____

(Use the most difficult word decoded correctly)
ML: "How did you know to say _____ that way?_____
_____
_____
_____

"Now, I'll say a word, and you make it for me." (*As you dictate, clearly articulate by "stretching" each sound. Example: tan = /t/ /ă/ /n/, stop after tad and ask the first ML and articulation questions.*)

↓tan	_____		plat	_____
*tad	_____		mape	_____
tap	_____		pridder	_____
leb	_____		radmin	_____

*ML: "How did you know to change [the 'n' to a 'd']? (*Use the letter changes the student has made.*)_____
_____

3

Articulation: "Tell me what my mouth did to help you spell _____ ." (*Repeat the most difficult word they spelled correctly.*) Record verbal responses and behaviors.

_____

_____

(Use the most difficult word spelled correctly)
ML: "How did you know to spell _____ that way?_____

_____

Words:
Lay out the collection of word cards [**I, me, the, a, is, at, look, dog, cat, big, map, can, sat, fat, sit, on, run**].
"I'll show you some words, and you read each one." (*Record, and if incorrect, say the right word,*)

I _____	me _____	the_____	a_____
is _____	at _____	look _____	dog _____
cat _____	big _____	map _____	can _____
sat _____	fat _____	sit _____	on _____
run _____			

Sentences:
"I'll make a sentence with some words, and you read the sentence for me."
I can run. _____
Look at me. _____
I sat on the cat. _____
The map is big. _____
_____
Sit the dog on the fat cat. _____

"Now I'll say a sentence, and you can make it for me." [Have the student read the sentence after building it.] (*Record sentence made and the student's read of it.*)

I can sit. _____
The dog is fat. _____
Look at the map. _____
A dog can look at me. _____
The big cat sat on the dog. _____
"Now I want you to read one sentence for me." (*Give the student the sheet with the sentence printed on it. Record the student's reading.*)

General Observations: _____

_____

_____

Tile Test Words

Copy this page cut (laminate) for use in word and sentence reading segments.

I | . | at | me | .

look | the | dog | a | .

cat | is | big | A | .

map | on | can | .

run | sat | Look | .

fat | Sit | sit | The

Graduated Running Record

The Graduated Running Record is an assessment that allows a teacher to systematically observe what a child does as he or she reads connected text aloud. It brings to the forefront the student's use of the semantic, syntactic, and graphophonemic cuing systems, enabling the teacher to quickly determine areas of strength and weakness.

The Graduated Running Record is formatted in a manner that minimizes the time commitment needed to individually assess an elementary class. Each version offers one paragraph on an interesting Social Studies, Science, or narrative topic. The Early Reading Format assesses young students' reading at the pre-primer/primer level. In the two Elementary Level Formats each of the seven sentences in the passage increases in difficulty from the previous sentence. Starting the passage at a mid-first grade level, the sentences advance in difficulty by grade, with the final sentence reflecting a sixth grade reading level. The average time needed to administer varies with the reading level of the child, but should not exceed 90 seconds. Since comprehension is jeopardized when fluency is poor, the 90 second stop limit is used as one criterion for ending the reading. A second stop limit is based on the number of grade level words missed in a sentence.

Teachers can evaluate each student's employment of the semantic, syntactic and graphophonemic cuing systems, aiding them to individualize instruction and promote optimal growth in reading. This knowledge is gained by evaluating the total amount of text read in the allotted time for fluency, the types of substitutions, omissions, and self corrections the child makes, and the level of expression and phrasing employed while reading the passage aloud to the teacher. Comprehension for each version is assessed by having the student retell the story. If the student does not finish the story in 90 seconds, then the test administrator reads the remaining portion of the story aloud to the child. When this occurs, both listening and reading comprehension can be evaluated with the retell.

GRADUATED RUNNING RECORD ADMINISTRATION GUIDE

The Graduated Running Record assesses accuracy, fluency, expression or prosody, and comprehension for the pre-primer and primer levels in the Early Reading Format, and the middle Grade One level to the Grade Six level in the Elementary Level Formats. In the Elementary Level Formats the first sentence is a measure of the middle Grade One level, while the second sentence assesses the reading level for the end of Grade One. Each of the following sentences advances a grade, with the third sentence at Grade Two and the last sentence assessing Grade Six. The Early Reading Format assesses young students' reading at the Pre-primer and Primer.

Directions:

Read the title of the passage to the student and direct him or her to read the passage aloud to you. Tell the student:

"The title of this story is _____. Now, I would like you to read this story aloud to me. Think about the story as you read it. After you finish reading, I will ask you to tell me what you remember from the story. As you read I will be making marks on my paper to help me remember what you say. The words in the story will be getting harder with each sentence. I may ask you to stop reading before you have finished the story. If you have not finished reading the story, I will read the rest of it to you."

Use the recording sheet to note everything the child says. Specific notations are used in the following manner:

Assessing Fluency

Accurate reading: Every word read correctly is denoted with a check mark (Y).

Repetition: (not to be counted as an error) Underline the repeated word, phrase, or sentence.

Substitutions: Use a caret (^) to indicate a substituted word. Write the substituted word above the caret. Substitutions are counted as errors.

Self-corrections: (not to be counted as an error) Write the incorrect pronunciation of the word. Then write SC above the word.

Omissions: Draw a line through an omitted word. Omissions are counted as errors. (If the student is trying to decode the word, let them continue. If they have given up on the word, tell the child the word.)

Stop rules:
1. Stop the assessment when the child has four or more errors **of underlined words only** in a sentence, **or**
2. if the child has not completed the story in 90 seconds or less.

***** If the student activates one of the stop criteria before reading to the end of the passage, then finish reading the rest of the passage to the child.

Determining the reading grade level: Note the sentence in which the student has made four or more errors, or where he or she was stopped due to the 90 second time limit. If the student is stopped in mid-sentence, then this partial sentence represents the student's frustration level. Reading grade level will be one grade level lower. For example, if frustration level was 3rd grade then the reading grade level will be 2nd grade reading level.

If the student completes the last sentence read, then that sentence indicates his reading grade level. For example, if the student finishes the last word in the fifth grade sentence as she reaches the 90 second cut-off point, and she has not misread four or five underlined words, then her reading level is fifth grade.

Calculating accuracy rate: Using only the UNDERLINED words on the recording sheet, count the total number of words read correctly. Then, count all of the underlined words to the point the student stopped reading.

Using only UNDERLINED words, calculate Accuracy Rate:

> # of Correct **Underlined** Words
> ──────────────────────────── X 100 = % of words read correctly
> Total Underlined Words to the stop point
>
> EXAMPLE: 63 underlined words read correctly
> ──────────────────────────── X 100 = 90% accuracy rate
> 70 underlined words to the stop point

Assessing Expression (Prosody)

Indicate the grade level of the last sentence in which the student has read most of the time with appropriate "flow" and phrasing as well as attended to punctuation with pauses and appropriate inflection. If the child does not read with appropriate expression or prosody, then score expression with a "0". For example, if the student reads through the second grade sentence with correct expression and continues through the fourth grade sentence before reaching the 90 second stop rule, then the score for expression is 2nd grade.

<u>Assessing Comprehension – The Retelling</u>

When the student has finished reading the passage or after you have finished reading the passage to the student, say to him, **"Please tell the story to me as if I had never heard it before."** On the recording sheet, 30 phrases or individual words are in bold type to indicate the main concepts of the passage. Twenty words or phrases are in bold for the Pre-primer/Primer level recording sheet. Listen for those words and phrases; **an approximation of the phrases should be considered correct.** Do not consider it an error if the retelling is somewhat out of order when comparing it to the actual text. Record the information that the student includes in the retelling on the right side of the recording sheet. You may prompt the student by saying, **"Can you tell me more?"** or **"What else do you remember?"** or by reminding him or her of the title of the passage.

Divide the number of concepts remembered by the student by the total number of concepts in the passage. Then, multiply by 100. That will give you the percentage of correct concepts remembered. The greater the percentage, the higher the comprehension level is. For example:

> 20 correct concepts retold
> ──────────────────────── X 100 = 66.7% comprehension of the passage
> 30 total concepts

(If the child read some of the passage, and you read the rest of the passage aloud to the child, you can compare the percentage of reading comprehension to the percentage of listening comprehension.)

The Good Dog

That dog is little and red. He is my pal. I call him Spot. Spot likes to play at my house, but then he runs away to his home up the hill.

Every day the children, who live around here, ask to see Spot. They think the dog is funny when he sprints past them to the plants and drops the stick that they tossed. On most days we all romp in the grass with Spot from sun-up to sunset.

Graduated Running Recording Sheet: Pre-primer / Primer Level

Student:_____**Teacher:**_____**School:**_____**Date:**_____

Underlined Words Correct_____ **Total Underlined Words** _____

Total time_____

Self-Corrections_____ **Omissions**_____ **Substitutions**_

End Sentence_____ **% Accuracy**_____ **Prosody**_____

Retell Score_____

Pre-primer:

The Good Dog

That dog is little and red. He_5 is my pal.

I call him $Spot_{10}$. Spot likes to play at my house,

but_{15} then he runs away to his $home_{20}$ up the hill.

Primer:

Every day_{25} the children, who live around

here, ask to see Spot. They $think_{30}$ the dog is funny

when he sprints past them to the $plants_{35}$ and drops

the stick that they tossed. On most days we all $romp_{40}$

in the grass with Spot from sun-up to $sunset_{45}$.

Retell

	NOTES

That **dog** is **little and red.**	1.
He is **my pal.**	2.
I call him **Spot.**	3.
Spot **likes to play** at my house, but then he **runs away to his home up the hill**	4.
Every day the children, **who live around here**, ask to **see Spot.**	5.
They think the **dog is funny** when he **sprints past**	6.
them **to the plants** and **drops the stick** that they tossed.	
On **most days** we all **romp in the grass with Spot** from **sun-up to sunset.**	7.

Retell
Score:

/

10

What made this a good place for a mother, father, and children to work and play? Many children who were living on this land a very long time ago slept at night in little huts. These small houses were made with reeds or branches and had places carefully made of stones for cooking the food the family found. Early each morning the hard-working people living together in the tiny village were ready to walk to different places looking for special foods. After gathering a variety of edible acorns and seeds using woven reed baskets, these women and girls of the settlement mashed their mounds of nuts into meal. Several men traveling by particular routes into the wilderness hunted the plentiful small prey such as squirrels, rabbits, and birds with nets, curved throwing sticks, or bows and arrows. Other adults rowed large wooden boats protected with tar to neighboring island settlements to trade for unique and nourishing sources of protein to expand their seafood diet.

Graduated Running Record Recording Sheet - Form A

Student:_____ Teacher:_____ School:_____ Date:_____

Underlined Words Correct_____ Total **Underlined Words** _____

Total time_____

Self-Corrections_____ Omissions_____ Substitutions_____

End Sentence_____ % Accuracy_____ Prosody_____

Retell Score_____

First Home

What made this a good place$_5$ for a mother, father, and children to work$_{10}$ and play? $\boxed{Mid\ 1st}$

Many children who were living on this land$_{15}$ a very long time ago slept at night in little huts$_{20}$. $\boxed{End\ 1^{st}}$

These small houses were made with reeds or branches and had places carefully$_{25}$ made of stones for cooking the food the family found. $\boxed{End\ 2^{nd}}$

Early$_{30}$ each morning the hard-working people living together$_{35}$ in the tiny village were ready to walk to different places looking for special$_{40}$ foods. $\boxed{End\ 3^{rd}}$

After gathering a variety of edible acorns and seeds using$_{45}$ woven reed baskets, these women and girls of the settlement mashed$_{50}$ their mounds of nuts into meal. $\boxed{End\ 4^{th}}$

Several men traveling by particular$_{55}$ routes into the wilderness hunted the plentiful small prey such as squirrels$_{60}$, rabbits, and birds with nets, curved throwing sticks, or bows and arrows$_{65}$. $\boxed{End\ 5^{th}}$

Other adults rowed large wooden boats protected with tar to neighboring$_{70}$ island settlements to trade for unique and nourishing sources of protein$_{75}$ to expand their seafood diet$_{78}$. $\boxed{End\ 6^{th}}$

Graduated Running Record Retell Form A

Name:_____ **Teacher:**_____ **School:**_____

First Home

What made this a **good place** for a **mother, father, and
children** to **work and play**?

Many children who were living on this land a very **long
time ago   slept**   at night **in little huts**.

These small **houses** were **made with reeds or
branches** and had places carefully made of **stones for
cooking** the food the family found.

Early each morning the **hard-working people** living
together **in the tiny village** were ready to **walk** to
different places **looking for special foods**.

After gathering a variety of edible **acorns and seeds**
using woven reed **baskets**, these **women and girls** of
the settlement **mashed their mounds of nuts** into meal.

Several **men** traveling by particular routes **into the
wilderness   hunted** the plentiful small prey such as
squirrels, rabbits, and birds with **nets, curved
throwing sticks, or bows and arrows**.

Other **adults   rowed large wooden boats** protected
with tar **to neighboring island** settlements **to trade** for
unique and nourishing **sources of protein** to expand
their **seafood diet**.

Retell:

1.

2.

3.

4.

5.

6.

7.

13

Retell
Score:

_____/30

Making Work Like Play

That man comes to this place to work and to play with his children. He thinks it's great to swim under the water to find many animals that live there. This morning he quietly noticed some light green fish eating insects that carefully landed on the blue water near the beach. As the seaside became more crowded, he swam to the entrance of another cove because he knew there would be hundreds of limpets covering the rough rocks along the shore. Here on the island's windward side, the ocean waves entered the cove's coral-guarded boundaries without a problem and then fought to escape to the freedom of the open sea again. From all indications, the shoreline explorer was convinced he would be astonished by the impressive number of oysters and other sea creatures living in the cove free from threatening pollution. In his role as a prominent marine biologist, he planned to conduct extensive research on the organisms found in this watery environment while vowing to protect it aggressively from inappropriate use by hostile commercial businesses.

Graduated Running Recording Sheet - Form B

Student:_____Teacher:_____School:_____Date:_____

Underlined Words Correct_____ Total **Underlined Words** _____

Total time_____

Self-Corrections_____ Omissions_____ Substitutions_____

End Sentence_____ % Accuracy_____ Prosody_____

Retell Score_____

Making Work Like Play

That man comes to this$_5$ place to work and to play with his children.$_{10}$ *Mid 1st*

He thinks it's great to swim under the water$_{15}$ to find many animals that live there.$_{20}$ *End 1st*

This morning he quietly noticed some light$_{25}$ green fish eating insects that carefully$_{30}$ landed on the blue water near the beach. *End 2nd*

As the seaside$_{35}$ became more crowded, he swam to the entrance of another$_{40}$ cove because he knew there would be hundreds of limpets$_{45}$ covering the rough rocks along the shore. *End 3rd*

Here on the island's$_{50}$ windward side, the ocean waves entered the cove's coral-guarded$_{55}$ boundaries without a problem and then fought to escape to the freedom$_{60}$ of the open sea again. *End 4th*

From all indications, the shoreline explorer was convinced$_{65}$ he would be astonished by the impressive number of oysters and other sea creatures$_{70}$ living in the cove free from threatening pollution. *End 5th*

In his role as a prominent marine biologist$_{75}$, he planned to conduct extensive research on the organisms$_{80}$ found in this watery environment while vowing to protect$_{85}$ it aggressively from inappropriate use by hostile commercial businesses$_{90}$. *End 6th*

Name:_____ Teacher:_____ School:_____

Making Work Like Play	Retell
That **man** comes to this place **to work** and **to play with his children**.	1.
He thinks **it's great** to **swim under the water** to **find many animals** that live there.	2.
This morning he quietly **noticed some light green fish eating insects** that carefully landed on the blue water **near the beach**.	3.
As the seaside became **more crowded**, he swam to the entrance of **another cove** because he knew there would be **hundreds of limpets** covering the rough rocks **along the shore**.	4.
Here on the island's **windward side**, the ocean waves entered **the cove's coral-guarded boundaries** without a problem and then **fought to escape** to the freedom of **the open sea again**.	5.
From all indications, the **shoreline explorer** was convinced he **would be astonished** by the impressive **number of oysters and other sea creatures** living in **the cove** free from **threatening pollution**.	6.
In his role as a prominent **marine biologist**, he planned to **conduct extensive research** on the **organisms found** in this watery environment while **vowing to protect** it aggressively from **inappropriate use** by hostile commercial **businesses**.	7.

Retell
Score:

_____/30

The Interactive Reading Assessment System – Revised

The Interactive Reading Assessment System – Revised (IRAS-R) is an informal reading inventory comprised of a set of subtests that is individually administered to determine a student's reading strengths and weaknesses. The skills tested include most of those generally accepted as necessary for success in skilled reading. The rationale for the array of tasks selected for IRAS-R rests on a theory of reading as a set of independent component skills (Calfee & Drum, 1979). By "independent" we mean that a student may have <u>relative</u> strengths or weaknesses within the several areas. The primary skill areas reflected in the tasks include decoding, vocabulary, grammar, understanding paragraphs and understanding longer passages (Calfee & Spector, 1981).

Overview of the System

IRAS is particularly suited to students past the initial primer level. The materials in the test are selected to cover a wide range of skills and knowledge in the areas of reading and oral language, from the level expected of a <u>midyear first grader</u> to that of a <u>junior high school student.</u>

If all subtests of the IRAS are selected, IRAS can be administered in one session of about 40 to 50 minutes, or in two sessions of approximately 30 minutes each. However, the system is designed to assess one or more skills as needed; a selection of appropriate subtests should be made to address the identified skills in question. If you are planning to administer the sight word and the comprehension tasks, use the word recognition/decoding first. Directions for administration are included at the beginning of each subtest.

<u>Decoding and word knowledge</u> is measured in four ways. First, students are asked to <u>read common sight words</u> within the student's reading vocabulary and beyond. Next, the student is asked to <u>define words</u>. Depending on how well he or she performs, the student is moved to lists of easier or more difficult words. Then, letter-sound correspondence is measured in two ways using <u>an alphabet recognition task</u> that asks for <u>letter identification and letter-sound relationships</u> and by having the student <u>read lists of synthetic words.</u> The synthetic words are divided into six categories according to the spelling pattern: vowels controlled by a final "e", vowels controlled by single and double consonants, vowel and consonant digraphs, vowel plus "r", segmented polysyllables, and polysyllabic words the student is asked to divide before reading. Finally, the student is <u>asked to spell or build</u> a list of phonetically regular synthetic words of increasing difficulty.

<u>Oral reading and comprehension</u> is assessed in several ways. The sentence reading and text passages roughly correspond to the sight word reading lists. First, the student is asked to read a <u>graded series of sentences to assess fluency.</u> The next sets of tasks includes reading <u>narrative and expository passages to assess comprehension.</u> The materials are designed to give students the opportunity to <u>read orally and silently.</u> Passages above students' reading ability are also included to assess students' <u>listening comprehension.</u> Comprehension is assessed with <u>a retelling of the passage</u> and <u>answering probe questions.</u>

INTERACTIVE READING ASSESSMENT SYSTEM
RECORDING SHEET

Student: _____ Teacher: _____ Grade: _____

Administrator: _____ School: _____ Date: _____

Age: _____ Circle one: Male   Female

First Language: English   Spanish   Other Specify: _____

	Raw Score	Grade Level
Alphabet Recognition: **# named**		
# sounds known		
Word Recognition / Decoding: Last list passed		
Meta-Linguistic Question: Rubric score		
Vocabulary: Last list passed		
Letter-Sound Correspondence (synthetic words): Last list passed		
Building synthetic words:___ # built		
Sentence Reading: Last sentence passed		
Reading Fluency		
Reading Comprehension		

Notes:_____

_____

_____

_____

_____

_____

_____

Alphabet Recognition:

Directions: Tester points to a letter, and says, "What is the name of this letter? What sound does it make?"

a   s   m   u   e   n

c   p   l   o   t   d

A   S   M   U   E   N

C   P   L   O   T   D

Decoding and Vocabulary Response Sheet

Directions:

I. Word Recognition / Decoding:

Show the first four lists to the student and ask which list is the most difficult one he/she can read. Begin with that list. Proceed through the lists until **4 or more errors** are made on one list. If 4 errors are made on the first list attempted, have the student try the previous list. Continue in this fashion until three or less errors are made. Once you have established the word recognition level proceed to Step II. Meta-Language.

II. Meta-Language:

Select the last word pronounced correctly. Ask the meta-language question:

"You were right when you said _____ for this word. How did you know to pronounce

(say) it that way?"

If the student is reluctant to answer, use probes such as:
"Have you seen that word before?" "Did it remind you of another word?" Do these letters or syllables help you? How?

III. Vocabulary:

Beginning with the decoding list on which the student failed, tell the student the first underlined word and ask for the definition. If the student is unable to define the word, use the accompanying prompt and place a check on the prompt line. Record the student's responses. Continue asking for the definitions of only the underlined words until the student is unable to define two underlined words on one list. If the student is unable to define the first word set attempted go back through the lists until the student is able to define at least two words.

Stop rule: Stop the Decoding portion at 4 or more errors in one list.
Stop the Vocabulary portion at 2 or more errors in one list.

Word List	Decoding	Prompt	Definition/Alternatives

X Grade Level: Early 1st

mud _____ _____ _____
a large bird, wet dirt, a book

pig _____ _____

its _____ _____

glad _____ _____ _____
sad, nervous, happy

sent _____ _____

top _____ _____ _____
A high place, inside a box, bottom

Y Grade Level: Early 1st

spent _____ _____

rub _____ _____ _____
To wash, to brush together, to bounce

basket _____ _____ _____
Something to hold things, to bounce, to drive

until _____ _____

them _____ _____

fist _____ _____ _____
A kind of dance, a way to hold your hand, a water animal

- Use only when the last correct list is reached.

- Select the hardest word pronounce correctly.

"You were right when you said _____ for this word. How did you know to pronounce (say) it that way?"_____

_____ _____

Stop rule: Stop the Decoding portion at 4 or more errors in one list.
　　　　　Stop the Vocabulary portion at 2 or more errors in one list.
A. Grade Level: Mid 1st

<u>end</u>	v.	_____	_____	_____
				to: stop, go slow, start
long		_____		
<u>little</u>	a.	_____	_____	_____
				something: large, tall, small
time		_____		
<u>house</u>	n.	_____	_____	_____
				animal to ride, place to live, bus stop
same		_____		

B. Grade Level: Late 1st

<u>food</u>	n.	_____	_____	_____
				something: to eat, to wear, to play
city		_____		
<u>best</u>	a.	_____	_____	_____
				something: as sweet as can be, as big as can be, as good as can be
paper		_____		
<u>tell</u>	v.	_____	_____	_____
				to: cry, say, yell
room		_____		

- Use only when the last correct list is reached.

- Select the hardest word pronounce correctly.

"You were right when you said _____ for this word. How did you know to

pronounce (say) it that way?"_____

_____

Stop rule: Stop the Decoding portion at 4 or more errors in one list.
           Stop the Vocabulary portion at 2 or more errors in one list.

C. Grade Level: Mid 2nd

fast a.   _____ _____   _____

                                          quick, loud, slow

black   _____

feel   v.   _____ _____   _____

                                          to: tease, taste, touch

table   _____

birds   n.   _____ _____   _____

                                          thorns on a bush, animals
                                          with feathers, animals with
                                          scales

cold   _____

D. Grade Level: End 2nd

music   n.   _____ _____   _____

                                          sound patterns, loud noises,
                                          twinkling lights

watch   _____

explain   v.   _____ _____   _____

                                          to: tell your name, count to
                                          ten, tell meaning

color   _____

heat   v.   _____ _____   _____

                                          to: burn, warm, go fast

machine   _____

- Use only when the last correct list is reached.

- Select the hardest word pronounce correctly.

"You were right when you said _____ for this word. How did you know to
pronounce (say) it that way?"_____

_____ _____

Stop rule: Stop the Decoding portion at 4 or more errors in one list.
Stop the Vocabulary portion at 2 or more errors in one list.

E. Grade Level: Mid 3rd

<u>skin</u>	n.	_____	_____	_____

outside of a balloon, outside of your body, inside of a grape

race		_____

<u>afraid</u>	a.	_____	_____	_____

surprised, frightened, successful

please		_____

<u>fight</u>	v.	_____	_____	_____

to: hit, break, fall

middle		_____

F. Grade Level: End 3rd

<u>hungry</u>	a.	_____	_____	_____

in a hurry, going away, wanting food

finger		_____

<u>visit</u>	v.	_____	_____	_____

to go: to see a friend, for a bus ride, to a show

electric		_____

<u>crowd</u>	n.	_____	_____	_____

kind of party, type of bird, lots of people

kitchen		_____

- Use only when the last correct list is reached.

- Select the hardest word pronounce correctly.

"You were right when you said _____ for this word. How did you know to pronounce (say) it that way?"_____

_____

Stop rule: Stop the Decoding portion at 4 or more errors in one list.
            Stop the Vocabulary portion at 2 or more errors in one list.

G. Grade Level: Mid 4th

<u>lonely</u>	a.	_____	_____	_____
				to: want friends, feel sad, wait for dinner
development		_____		
<u>ability</u>	n.	_____	_____	_____
				a kind of: test, skill, award
honor		_____		
<u>observe</u>	v.	_____	_____	_____
				to: see through, look at, light up
industry		_____		

H. Grade Level: End 4th

<u>committee</u>	n.	_____	_____	_____
				people who: meet, have a party, build a house
atom		_____		
<u>delicate</u>	a.	_____	_____	_____
				breakable, soft, round
judge		_____		
<u>prevent</u>	v.	_____	_____	_____
				to: stop, allow, pretend
mission		_____		

- Use only when the last correct list is reached.

- Select the hardest word pronounce correctly.

"You were right when you said _____ for this word. How did you know to pronounce (say) it that way?"_____

_____ _____

Stop rule: Stop the Decoding portion at 4 or more errors in one list.
           Stop the Vocabulary portion at 2 or more errors in one list.

I.   Grade Level: Mid 5th

<u>issue</u>   v.   _____   _____   _____

                                                    (as a <u>verb</u>) to: order, give, refuse

muscle   _____

<u>annual</u>   a.   _____   _____   _____

                                                    lately, monthly, yearly

curiosity   _____

<u>literature</u>   v.   _____   _____   _____

                                                    kinds of writing, bag of trash, scratch paper

permanent   _____

J.   Grade Level: End 5th

<u>decade</u>   n.   _____   _____   _____

                                                    several days, ten years, two weeks

bomb   _____

<u>promptly</u>   adv.   _____   _____   _____

                                                    helpfully, in a hurry, right away

grease   _____

<u>demonstrate</u>   v.   _____   _____   _____

                                                    to: experiment, demand, show

extensive   _____

- Use only when the last correct list is reached.

- Select the hardest word pronounce correctly.

"You were right when you said _____ for this word. How did you know to pronounce (say) it that way?"_____

_____   _____

Stop rule: Stop the Decoding portion at 4 or more errors in one list.
 Stop the Vocabulary portion at 2 or more errors in one list.

K. Grade Level: Mid 6th

<u>deserve</u>   v.   _____ _____ _____
                                                     to have the: need, wish, right

retain   _____

<u>consequence</u> n.   _____ _____ _____
                                                     outcome, failure, lie

graduation   _____

<u>ominous</u>   a.   _____ _____ _____
                                                     threatening, shocking, appealing

skyscraper   _____

L. Grade Level: End 6th

<u>proclaim</u>   v.   _____ _____ _____
                                                     to: shout, deny, announce

elegance   _____

<u>controversial</u> a.   _____ _____ _____
                                                     agreeable, debatable,
                                                     doubtful

astute   _____

<u>aroma</u>   n.   _____ _____ _____
                                                     pleasant smell, pretty sunset,
                                                     spicy taste

implement   _____

- Use only when the last correct list is reached.

- Select the hardest word pronounce correctly.

"You were right when you said _____ for this word. How did you know to
pronounce (say) it that way?"_____

_____ _____

Stop rule: Stop the Decoding portion at 4 or more errors in one list.
　　　　　 Stop the Vocabulary portion at 2 or more errors in one list.

M.　Grade Level: Mid 7th

pessimistic　a.　＿＿＿＿＿＿　＿＿＿＿＿　＿＿＿＿＿＿＿＿＿＿＿

gloomy, worried, happy

dormant　　　　＿＿＿＿＿＿

boredom　　n.　＿＿＿＿＿＿　＿＿＿＿＿　＿＿＿＿＿＿＿＿＿＿＿

drowsiness, activity,
monotony

prudent　　　　＿＿＿＿＿＿

illuminate　v.　＿＿＿＿＿＿　＿＿＿＿＿　＿＿＿＿＿＿＿＿＿＿＿

to: burn, light up, destroy

frustration　　＿＿＿＿＿＿

N.　Grade Level: End 7th

mandatory　a.　＿＿＿＿＿＿　＿＿＿＿＿　＿＿＿＿＿＿＿＿＿＿＿

required, permitted, released

flamboyant　　＿＿＿＿＿＿

traverse　　v.　＿＿＿＿＿＿　＿＿＿＿＿　＿＿＿＿＿＿＿＿＿＿＿

veritable　　　＿＿＿＿＿＿

anthology　　n.　＿＿＿＿＿＿　＿＿＿＿＿　＿＿＿＿＿＿＿＿＿＿＿

collection of stories, study of
man, humorous saying

tumultuous　　＿＿＿＿＿＿

- Use only when the last correct list is reached.

- Select the hardest word pronounce correctly.

"You were right when you said ＿＿＿＿＿＿＿ for this word. How did you know to

pronounce (say) it that way?"＿＿＿＿＿＿＿＿＿＿＿＿＿＿＿＿＿＿＿＿＿＿＿＿＿＿＿

＿＿＿＿＿＿＿＿＿＿＿＿＿＿＿＿＿＿＿＿＿＿＿＿＿＿＿＿＿＿＿＿＿＿＿＿＿＿＿

Decoding Synthetic Words Lists:

Directions: Stop at **four or more** errors in one list and ask the meta-linguistic question at the bottom of the page. (List E is read as blended words. Words in List F are read first as separate syllables and then blended.)

<u>**Word List A**</u>

hin _____

nelp _____

flass _____

scrong _____

pame _____

vute _____

<u>**Word List B**</u>

shile _____

throve _____

snay _____

toin _____

spawk _____

spleek _____

<u>**Word List C**</u>

clur _____

derb _____

folp _____

sark _____

shald _____

plair _____

<u>**Word List D**</u>

worch _____

knop _____

ceft _____

flage _____

wrudge _____

glies _____

<u>**Word List E**</u>

lod-ded _____

fen-ing _____

wem-bick _____

lude-ful _____

un-fro-ten _____

im-pen-tive _____

af-fre-mi-a-tion _____

syn-thod _____

an-a-phen-ist _____

<u>**Word List F**</u>

jemming _____

saped _____

rimple _____

befade _____

dacture _____

conspartable _____

rhosmic _____

paraplast _____

euchormonium _____

Meta-linguistic question:
"You were right when you said _____ for this word. How did you know to pronounce (say) it that way?" _____

Possible prompts: Have you seen the word before? Did it remind you of another word?

Word Building (Spelling): Synthetic Words

     If available lay out the appropriate letter tiles for student word building activities. If letter tiles are not available use pencil and paper.

"Now, I'm going to say some funny pretend words and I want you to say the word after me. Then I want you to build the word for me." If the student misspells the word, continue through the set of three until one word is spelled correctly. If none are spelled correctly, stop.

A.   1. dut (but)   _____

         2. mape (cape)   _____

         3. leb (web)   _____

B.   4. fening (screening)   _____

         5. sidded (bid..)   _____

         6. javes (caves)   _____

C.   7. broint (joint)   _____

         8. glire (fire)   _____

         9. grotious (ferocious)   _____

D.   10. frintle (mint..)   _____

         11. choober (goober)   _____

         12. pridder (grid...)   _____

E.   13. strandister (stand..sister) _____

         14. closterish (roster..wish)   _____

         15. thrinkerlant (thinker..land) _____

Meta-linguistic question:

"You were right when you spelled this word _____. How did you know to spell it that way?_____

_____

Sentence Reading:

Directions: Stop when the student fails to read a minimum of **one highlighted** word correctly or when student takes more than 20 seconds to read a set of sentences. Score 1 point for each completed sentence, ½ point for partial success (only one highlighted word read correctly).

A.   I **LIKE** to **PLAY.**
     I like to eat a **RED** apple.

B.   Ann wants Mom to **MAKE** a **CAKE.** Mom cannot do it. She has to go to **WORK.**

C.   The man made the light **SHINE.** Right away Ed saw the baby **FOX** on top of its **CAGE.**

D.   The kitten was **SCARED** and climbed up the tree. The girl tried to **REACH** it but she had no **LUCK.**

E.   Jeff was **AFRAID** that he would miss the first act. As soon as he bought the **POPCORN**, he **HURRIED** to find Rose.

F.   About three miles from the **HARBOR**, Ray's boat was **CAUGHT** in an unexpected current. He spotted a tiny **ISLAND** and realized that he was approaching its shore.

G.   Harriet made many heroic **ATTEMPTS** to lead other slaves to freedom in the North. Her courage and **DETERMINATION** made her an **IMPORTANT** figure in the nation's history.

H.   Slowly the women **ASCENDED** the steep and icy **MOUNTAIN.** There were times when the sheer cliffs and the bitter cold **DISCOURAGED** them, but they would not relent.

Passage Reading

After studying the IRAS Passage Reading format, teachers are encouraged to create similar grade level passages with retelling and probe recording sheets from materials in the level book sets typically found in today's classrooms.

First, the student enters the passage reading subtest at the starting point indicated by his Sentence Reading performance. If the student reads the sentence set at Level C with adequate speed and accuracy, but cannot meet these criteria for Level D, then he should begin with Oral Reading Comprehension, Narrative C 1.

The student begins with either the Oral or Silent Reading task, depending on his entering level. If he cannot read Sentence Set X or A, or if he failed Word List A, then he should go immediately to Listening Comprehension, Narrative A2.

At each passage level, the student is tested on the narrative passage first, then the expository passage at the same level. Most students will find the narrative structure easier to comprehend than the expository structure.

Stop Rules:
For oral reading, the task is ended whenever the student exceeds 100 seconds to read a passage. Time is the only criterion; comprehension is not taken into account.

For silent reading and listening:
1. The student has succeeded at the retelling task if he passes half or more of the designated items.

2. The student has passed an element if he at least mentions it briefly.

The guiding principle in this task, as elsewhere in IRAS, is to give the student the benefit of the doubt and move onward to a more difficult task whenever possible.

Fluency and Comprehension:
Record times for reading only

TIME START		Response		Probe Questions
		Retell	Probe	

_____

Setting	It is a sunny day. ANN is on her bike.			
1. Goal₁	TOM WANTS to PLAY BALL			
Attempt₁	He ASKS ANN to PLAY with him	_____	_____	What did Tom want Ann to do?
2. Outcome₁ Initiating event₂	She will NOT PLAY ball now She WANTS to RIDE	_____	_____	What did Ann want to do (. . . when Tom asked her to play?)
Reaction₂	TOM is SAD			
3. Attempt₂	He ASKS Ann, "Can we take a RIDE and THEN PLAY BALL?	_____	_____	What did Tom say to Ann? (. . . when she didn't want to play ball)
4. Outcome₂	"YES" SAYS ANN. "That will be fun"			
Resolution	So TOM GETS his BIKE and THEY PLAY	_____	_____	How did story end?

TIME STOP

_____

Oral Reading
Comprehension/Nar A1

33

		Response		Probe Questions
		Retell	Probe	
Setting	JILL HAS a TREE HOUSE			
1.				
Goal$_1$	She WANTS to PAINT IT green			
				What did Jill want
Attempt$_1$	She ASKS SAM to HELP	_____	_____	Sam to do?
2.				
Outcome$_1$	SAM CANNOT help			What was Sam going
	He is GOING OUT with Pat			to do? (. . .when Jill
		_____	_____	asked him to help)
Initiating event$_2$				
Reaction$_2$	JILL is SAD			
3.				
Attempt$_2$	She ASKS DAD, "CAN YOU			
	come out and HELP me?"	_____	_____	What did Jill ask
				Dad?
4.				
Outcome$_2$	"YES," SAYS DAD. "I will help			
	you paint the tree house."			
Resolution	So JILL goes to GET the green			How did the story
	PAINT	_____	_____	end?

Listening
Comprehension/Nar A2

34

		Response		
		Retell	Probe	Probe Questions

Setting	PAM LIVED in a house BY a HILL.			
1. Initiating event₁	One morning she TOOK her brown BALL to the TOP of the HILL. The GRASS was WET and Pam FELL. The BALL ROLLED DOWN the HILL.	_____	_____	How did the story begin? (What happened when Pam took her ball to the top of the hill?)
Reaction	PAM began to CRY			
2. Attempt₁	She RAN AFTER IT	_____	_____	What did Pam do when the ball began to roll?
3. Outcome₁	but she COULD NOT STOP it. She SAW it FALL into a POND.	_____	_____	Where did the ball land?
4. Initiating event₂	Then a BOY WALKED by the POND. He SAW SOMETHING in the WATER.			
Attempt₂	PAM SAID, "TRY to GET my BALL"	_____	_____	What happened after the ball fell in pond? (What did Pam ask the boy to do?)
5. Outcome₂	The BOY JUMPED into the cold WATER. He GOT Pam's BALL.	_____	_____	What did the boy do?
6. Resolution	PAM THANKED him and then WALKED up the hill and PLAYED.	_____	_____	How did the story end?

Oral Reading
Comprehension/NAR B1

35

		Response		
		Retell	Probe	Probe Questions

Setting	ED WORKS AT the ZOO in town			
1. Initiating event₁	One night he TOOK some FOOD TO the baby FOX. He went TO its CAGE, but the FOX was NOT THERE			How did story begin? (What happened when Ed took food to the baby fox?
Reaction	ED was SURPRISED	_____	_____	
2. Attempt₁	He LOOKED AROUND, but he DID NOT SEE it.	_____	_____	What did Ed do when he found that the fox was missing?
3. Outcome₁	The FOX HID in the DARK	_____	_____	Why did Ed not see the fox?
4. Initiating event₂	Then a MAN WALKED by He HAD a LIGHT			
Attempt₂	ED SAID, "SHINE the LIGHT on the CAGE." The MAN made the LIGHT SHINE	_____	_____	What happened after fox hid in the dark? (What did Ed ask the man to do?)
5. Outcome₂	Right away Ed SAW the baby FOX on TOP of its CAGE	_____	_____	Where did they find the fox?
6. Resolution	So he PUT it BACK IN the CAGE and GAVE it some FOOD	_____	_____	How did story end?

Listening
Comprehension/Nar B2

		Response		Probe Questions
		Retell	Probe	
1.	BILL was DRESSED for WINTER. He had on a ROUND, FUR HAT. It was PULLED down OVER his EARS.	_____	_____	What was Bill's hat like?
2.	His long COAT was BUTTONED up TO his CHIN.	_____	_____	How was his coat buttoned?
3.	The BUTTONS were BIG and RED. They made him look LIKE a CLOWN	_____	_____	What did his buttons look like?
4.	Yes, Bill was DRESSED FOR the COLD. He had on his fur hat and his long coat. BUT his SHOES were all WET. I laughed when he HOPPED up and down to KEEP his FEET WARM.	_____	_____	Why did Bill have to hop up and down?

Listening
Comprehension/Exp B2

Response

Retell Probe

1. You should see ANN'S DOG. His name is
    Ed. He is BIGGER THAN ANN. She
    thinks he is getting bigger and BIGGER
    ALL THE TIME.

2. His COAT is RED, but the HAIR on his
    HEAD is dark BROWN.

3. He has LONG THIN LEGS and BIG FAT
    FEET. He has a BIG NOSE, too.

4. Ann thinks HE is funny. He can RUN like a
    RABBIT, but he EATS like a PIG.

Probe Questions
How big is Ann's
dog?

_____ _____

What is odd about
Ed's hair? (What
color is his
coat? / his head?)

_____ _____

What do Ed's
legs, feet, and
nose look like?

_____ _____

Why does Ann
think Ed is funny?
(How does he
run?) (How does
he eat?)

_____ _____

TIME STOP

_____

Oral Reading
Comprehension/Exp B1

<u>TIME START</u>

		Response		
		<u>Retell</u>	<u>Probe</u>	<u>Probe Questions</u>

Setting — Once there was an old MAN who LIVED BY a RIVER. It was WINTER and the RIVER was COVERED with ICE

1.
Initiating event₁ — One day he looked out his window and SAW a BOY by the river. The boy started to WALK ACROSS the river on the ICE   _____ _____   What were the man and the boy doing at the beginning of story?

Reaction — The old MAN was AFRAID that the ICE would BREAK

2.
Attempt₁ — He opened the window and CALLED out to the boy

Outcome₁ — But the BOY DIDN'T HEAR him, and he just KEPT on GOING   _____ _____   What happened when the old man saw the boy walk on the ice? (What did the man do?) (What did the boy do?)

3.
Initiating event₂ — When he got to the middle the ICE BROKE, and the BOY FELL into the WATER   _____ _____   What happened when the boy got to the middle of the river?

4.
Attempt₂ — The old MAN GOT a long LADDER and ran down to the river. He SLID the ladder ACROSS the ICE.   _____ _____   What did the man do when the boy feel in?

5.
Outcome₂ — The BOY GRABBED the LADDER and the MAN PULLED him OUT   _____ _____   How was the boy saved?

6.
Resolution — The next day the BOY visited the old man and THANKED him for saving his life   _____ _____   How did story end?

<u>TIME STOP</u>

_____

Oral Reading/Comprehension/Nar C1

39

	Response		
	Retell	Probe	Probe Questions

1. One way to MAKE MONEY in the summer is to SELL LEMONADE

_____ _____ How can you make money in the summer?

2. It is easy to make. You NEED LEMONS, WATER, SUGAR, and ICE.

_____ _____ What do you need to make lemonade?

3. PUT the JUICE from TEN LEMONS into TEN CUPS of WATER. ADD TWO CUPS of SUGAR and lots of ICE. Then stir it.

_____ _____ How do you make lemonade?

4. When you have the lemonade GET some PAPER CUPS and enough MONEY to make CHANGE. Also get a SMALL TABLE to put things on.

_____ _____ What things do you need to get beside lemonade?

5. The FIND a SPOT to set up. The CORNER of a STREET is GOOD.

_____ _____ Where is a good spot to set up your table?

6. When it GETS HOT, PEOPLE will stop to BUY a DRINK.

_____ _____ When will people stop to buy a drink?

Listening
Comprehension/Exp C2

		Response		
		Retell	Probe	Probe Questions
Setting	Once there was a little GIRL who HAD a KITTEN. The KITTEN liked to PLAY in the YARD by a tall tree			
1. Initiating event₁	Early one morning a dog was walking in front of the house. It was windy and the gate blew open. The DOG RAN INTO the YARD. The KITTEN was SCARED and RAN UP the TREE.	_____	_____	What happened at the beginning of the story?
2. Attempt₁ / Outcome₁	The GIRL TRIED to REACH it, but she had NO LUCK. The KITTEN CLIMBED to the HIGHEST BRANCH	_____	_____	What happened when the kitten ran up the tree? (what happened when the girl tried to reach the kitten?)
3. Initiating event₂	The girl's SISTER SAW the kitten FROM her WINDOW	_____	_____	What did the girl's sister see?
4. Attempt₂	She OPENED the window and LEANED OUT. She COULD REACH the BRANCH. "COME INSIDE," she SAID softly.	_____	_____	How did the sister try to save the kitten?
5. Outcome₂	She REACHED out when the KITTEN came closer. The she PULLED it INTO the HOUSE	_____	_____	What happened when the kitten came near the window?
6. Resolution	The night the little GIRL TOLD everyone WHAT HAPPENED. She was GLAD that her SISTER had SAVED the KITTEN	_____	_____	How did story end?

Listening
Comprehension/Nar C2

		Response		
		Retell	Probe	Probe Questions

1. It is easy to MAKE BUTTER. First you NEED a JAR and some heavy CREAM.

_____ _____ What do you need to make butter?

2. FILL the JAR PART way with CREAM. Then SHAKE it for about 20 MINUTES.

_____ _____ What is the first thing you do?

3. SOON the CREAM will start to get LUMPY. STOP WHEN most of the cream turns into LUMPS. You will find that the LUMPS are BUTTER.

_____ _____ When should you stop shaking the cream?

4. Take the lumps out of the jar and WASH them with COLD WATER.

_____ _____ What do you do with the lumps in the jar?

5. Mix a little SALT with the lumps of butter and PAT them TOGETHER. Leave the butter in a COOL PLACE over night.

_____ _____ After you wash the butter, what do you do?

6. In the morning the BUTTER will be HARD and READY to EAT.

_____ _____ How do you know when the butter is ready to eat?

Oral Reading
Comprehension/Exp C1

		Response	
		Retell Probe	Probe Questions

Setting₁ — JOE and his daughter SUE were FISHING at the LAKE.

1.
Initiating event₁ — They were THERE for an HOUR and had NOT CAUGHT any FISH.

Goal₁ — JOE WANTED to find a BETTER SPOT so he started to WALK

Attempt₁ — AROUND the LAKE.

2.
Outcome / — He PASSED a few FISHERMEN NEAR the DOCK. They TOLD HIM that they were CATCHING LOTS of FISH.

Initiating event₂

Reaction₂ — JOE was EXCITED to hear the news.

3.
Attempt₂ — and he STARTED BACK to GET his DAUGHTER.
Meanwhile SUE was FISHING by HERSELF.

Setting₃
4.
Initiating event₃ — She GOT TIRED and FELL ASLEEP with the pole in her hand.

5.
Development₃ — She slept until she FELT a strong TUG on her line
She was STARTLED to find that the fishing ROD was being PULLED INTO the WATER

Reaction₃

6.
Attempt₃ — Sue RUSHED INTO the LAKE just as her FATHER RETURNED

7.
Outcome₃ — Then she GRABBED the fishing POLE and PULLED it OUT of the water

8.
Resolution — BOTH Joe and Sue were AMAZED to discover an enormous FISH hooked ON the LINE.

Probe Questions:
- How did the story begin? (Why did Joe want to find another spot to fish?) (What did he do then?)
- What happened when Joe started to walk around the lake? (What did the fishermen tell him?)
- What did Joe do after he talked to the fishermen?
- What happened when Sue was fishing by herself?
- What woke Sue up?
- What did Sue do as her father returned?
- What did Sue do (.. when she ran into the lake?)
- How did the story end?

Oral Reading
Comprehension/Nar D1

		Response		
		Retell	Probe	Probe Questions

		Retell	Probe	Probe Questions
Setting₁	KATE and her cousin, JEFF, WENT to the CIRCUS. They arrived a half-hour before the afternoon show			
1. Goal₁	KATE WANTED to find GOOD SEATS			
Attempt₁ Outcome₁	She WALKED inside and SAW two empty SEATS in the FIRST ROW	____	_____	What did Kate do at the beginning?
2. Initiating event₂	but a LADY TOLD her that the SEATS were TAKEN	____	_____	What happened when she tried to find good seats?
Reaction₂	KATE was UNHAPPY because the front rows were already filled	____	_____	
3. Attempt₂	She WALKED TO the BACK to FIND two SEATS	____	_____	What did Kate do when the lady told her that the seats were taken?
Setting₂	Meanwhile, JEFF was WAITING in line AT the CANDY STAND	____	_____	
4. Initiating event₃	He WANTED to get some POPCORN before the show began	____	_____	Why was Jeff waiting in line at the candy stand?
Goal₃ 5. Developments₃	Suddenly he HEARD the BAND begin to PLAY	____	_____	What happened while Jeff was waiting in line?
Reaction₃ 6. Attempt₃	He WAS AFRAID that he would MISS the FIRST ACT			
	As soon as he BOUGHT the POPCORN he HURRIED to find Kate	____	_____	What did Jeff do when he heard the band begin to play?
7. Outcome₃	ON the WAY to his seat, he TRIPPED and SPILLED the POPCORN	____	_____	What happened to Jeff on the way to his seat?
8. Resolution	Finally, he FOUND his COUSIN IN the BACK ROW and THEY began to WATCH the SHOW. They DIDN'T HAVE GOOD SEATS and they didn't have any POPCORN, but they ENJOYED the CIRCUS anyway	____	_____	How did story end?

Listening
Comprehension/Nar D2

		Response		
		Retell	Probe	Probe Questions

1.   Not far from where I live there is an old CASTLE. It is NOT very BIG. It is made of GRAY STONES and has a TOWER on one SIDE of the MAIN BUILDING.   _____   _____   What does the castle look like?

2.   The TOWER is ROUND and about <u>30</u> FEET TALL.   _____   _____   What does the tower look like?

3.   There is a LONG NARROW WINDOW near the TOP. The GLASS in the window has been BROKEN for many years.   _____   _____   What does the window in the tower look like?

4.   There is a CELLAR HOLE on the OTHER SIDE of the castle.   _____   _____   What is on the other side of the castle?

5.   It is FILLED with ROCKS and WEEDS. Some WOOD also remains FROM the BARN that used to be there.   _____   _____   What is in the cellar hole?

6.   It is EASY to TELL that NO ONE has LIVED there for a long time. Even the ROAD is GROWN OVER with GRASS.   _____   _____   How can you tell that no one has lived there for a long time?

Listening
Comprehension/Exp D2

Response

	Retell	Probe	Probe Questions

1.   There is a big old TREE in the yard outside my window. It is STRAIGHT and TALL and looks LIKE a CONE.   ____   ____   What shape is the tree?

2.   The BRANCHES at the BOTTOM are WIDE and FULL.   ____   ____   What are the bottom branches like?

3.   The tree GOES way ABOVE the ROOF of my house.   ____   ____   How high does the tree go?

4.   At the TOP it is NARROW and comes to a POINT.   ____   ____   What is the tree like at the top?

5.   The green LEAVES that cover its branches are NOT REALLY LEAVES at all. They are SHARP and POINTED and make me think of NEEDLES.   ____   ____   What are the leaves like?

6.   The tree in my yard is ALWAYS GREEN. In winter the other trees lose their leaves. But even when snow falls and it is cold I can look at my tree and think of spring.   ____   ____   What is the tree like in winter?

_____

Oral Reading
Comprehension/Exp D1

		Response		
		Retell	Probe	**Probe Questions**

Setting	The moon had just risen as JAN looked toward the old deserted house.			
1. Goal₁	She was WAITING for her FRIEND, Ellen. Together they PLANNED to FIND out IF the HOUSE was HAUNTED.	_____	_____	How did the story begin? (Why were Jan and Ellen meeting by the old house?)
2. Initiating event₁	When ELLEN ARRIVED the two friends began to WALK nervously UP the PATH. A strange SHADOW seemed to FALL ACROSS the WINDOW next to the porch.	_____	_____	What did the girls do right after Ellen arrived? (What happened as they walked up the path?)
Reaction₁ 3. Attempt₁	Both GIRLS were SCARED, but they pretended not to notice. Then as ELLEN HELD the FLASHLIGHT, JAN anxiously pushed OPEN the DOOR.			
Outcome₁	Once INSIDE the house they were STARTLED to HEAR a peculiar SCRATCHING SOUND	_____	_____	What did the girls hear when they entered the house?
Initiating event₂ 4. Attempt₂	ELLEN FLASHED her LIGHT all around	_____	_____	What did Ellen do when she heard the scratching sound?
5. Outcome₂	but she could NOT FIND where the SOUND was coming from.	_____	_____	Did they find where the sound was coming from?
6. Initiating event₃	But it seemed to be COMING TOWARD THEM. Suddenly JAN felt SOMETHING RUB against her LEG.	_____	_____	What happened to Jan?
Reaction₃	She TRIED to SCREAM but was too SCARED to make a sound.			
7. Attempt₃	She GRABBED ELLEN'S ARM and stared at her in shock. ELLEN FLASHED the LIGHT her way, and then	_____	_____	What did Ellen do when Jan grabbed her arm?
8. Outcome₃	they both REALIZED WHAT was HAUNTING the HOUSE. It was just an old BLACK CAT who had made the house its home.			
Resolution		_____	_____	What did the girls discover in the end?

Silent Reading/Comprehension/Nar E1

		Response Retell	Probe	Probe Questions
Setting 1.	It was LATE AFTERNOON.			
Initiating event₁	ALICE STOOD by the OPEN BARN DOOR. She had LATCHED the door this MORNING, but NOW it was OPEN and her HORSE, Sam, was MISSING.	_____	_____	How did story begin? (Why was it odd that the door was open?)
Reaction₁	Alice FEARED that SAM would NOT RETURN before nightfall			
2. Attempt₁	So she DECIDED to go LOOK for him.	_____	_____	What did Alice do when she found that Sam was missing?
3. Outcome₁ Initiating event₂ Reaction₂	A short way from the barn she SPOTTED Sam GRAZING in a PASTURE, but he was not alone. ANOTHER HORSE from a neighbor's farm was alongside him. ALICE was SURPRISED to see the other horse.	_____	_____	What did Alice see in the picture?
4. Attempt₂	She GOT two ROPES and WENT into the pasture AFTER the HORSES	_____	_____	How did Alice try to catch the horses?
5. Outcome₂	When she finally caught both of them, Alice PUT SAM back IN the BARN.	_____	_____	When she caught him, what did Alice do with Same?
6. Initiating event₃ Reaction₃	Then she TRIED to TIE the OTHER horse TO a nearby POST, BUT he BROKE LOOSE from her grasp. ALICE was beginning to get ANGRY.	_____	_____	What happened after Alice got Sam back in the barn?
7. Attempt₃	She TRIED to CATCH the HORSE again, but before she could reach him, he RAN to the BARN and LIFTED the LATCH WITH his NOSE	_____	_____	What happened when Alice tried to catch the other horse? (What did other horse do after he broke away?)
8. Outcome₃ Resolution	Suddenly Alice REALIZED why the DOOR had been OPEN. The neighbor's HORSE had LET SAM OUT.	_____	_____	Why was the barn door open all this time?

Listening
Comprehension/Nar E2

		Response		Probe
		Retell	Probe	Questions
1.	A GROUP of students is PLANNING to start a NATURE CLUB.	_____	_____	What are some students planning to do?
2.	Anyone INTERESTED in WILD ANIMALS, BIRDS, PLANTS, or WILDERNESS HIKING is INVITED to join. NO membership FEE will be charged.	_____	_____	What is told about joining the club?
3.	The CLUB is being FORMED in order to COMBINE the INTERESTS of several SMALLER GROUPS.	_____	_____	Why is the club being formed?
4.	In the past, these GROUPS have NOT had ENOUGH MEMBERS to BECOME official SCHOOL CLUBS. At least TWENTY members are NEEDED to MEET school REQUIREMENTS.	_____	_____	What problems have some groups had in forming clubs?
5.	There are several BENEFITS to having an OFFICIAL CLUB. The SCHOOL PROVIDES an adult ADVISOR, MONEY for activities, and HELP in PLANNING FIELD TRIPS. It provides OFFICE space and ALLOWS the club to hold MEETINGS DURING SCHOOL hours.	_____	_____	What are the benefits of having an official club?
6.	Without these BENEFITS it is DIFFICULT for groups to FUNCTION.	_____	_____	Why are the benefits important?

ListeningComprehension/Exp E2

		Response		Probe
		Retell	Probe	Questions

1. An AMUSEMENT PARK is OPENING in town next Saturday.

_____ _____   What is happening on Saturday?

2. There will be a PARADE, FIREWORKS, and FREE ADMISSION on opening day. More than FIVE THOUSAND PEOPLE are EXPECTED to attend.

_____ _____   What will opening day be like?

3. WORK first began on the park TWO YEARS ago. At that time the SITE WAS an UNUSED FIELD. It was FILLED with WEEDS and TRASH. Although occasional ATTEMPTS had been made to CLEAN it up, NOTHING had WORKED.

_____ _____   What did the site of the park used to look like?

4. SINCE then more than FIFTY RIDES, a PLAYHOUSE, and a PICNIC GROUND have been built. Many TREES and BUSHES also have been PLANTED.

_____ _____   What is the park like now?

5. After opening day, ADMISSION to the park will cost THREE DOLLARS. However, CHILDREN UNDER TWELVE will be let in FREE IF they come WITH an ADULT.

_____ _____   What about admission to the park?

6. All RIDES will cost FIFTY CENTS, except the ROLLERCOASTER, which will cost a DOLLAR.

_____ _____   How much will rides be?

Silent Reading
Comprehension/Exp E1

		Response		Probe
		Retell	Probe	Questions

Setting | It was the year <u>1849</u> in the small town of BUCKSTOWN, MARYLAND

1.
Goal₁ | A Young, black SLAVE, named Harriet Tubman, DECIDED to ESCAPE from the SOUTH and SEEK her FREEDOM. Harriet AWAITED a CHANCE to begin the trip NORTHWARD. | _____ _____ | What did Harriet want to do at beginning?

2.
Initiating event₁ | One evening a farmer VOLUNTEERED to HIDE Harriet in his CART underneath a LOAD of VEGETABLES. | _____ _____ | How did the farmer help Harriet?

Reaction | Harriet was TERRIFIED that she would be CAUGHT trying to escape, but she was DETERMINED to take the RISK.

3.
Attempt₁ | Harriet TRAVELED on a ROUTE known as the UNDERGROUND RAILROAD. The underground was not a real railroad, but an ORGANIZATION of people who PROVIDED rides and hiding places for slaves ESCAPING from PLANTATIONS in the South. | _____ _____ | What route did Harriet travel?

4.
Elaboration (definition) | | _____ _____ | What was the underground railroad?

5.
Outcome₁ | Harriet spent several exhausting NIGHTS traveling. Finally she ARRIVED at the PENNSYLVANIA border. She was a FREE citizen for the first time in her life. | _____ _____ | Tell about Harriet's trip. (How did it end?)

6.
Resolution | AFTERWARD, Harriet made many HEROIC ATTEMPTS to LEAD other SLAVES to FREEDOM in the North. Because of her COURAGE and DETERMINATION she is an important FIGURE in the NATION'S HISTORY. | _____ _____ | Why is Harriet an important figure in the nation's history?

Silent Reading
Comprehension/Nar F1

		Response		Probe
		Retell	Probe	Questions

Setting
It was WINTER in the town of KITTY HAWK, NORTH CAROLINA

1.
Goal
This was the day WILBUR and ORVILLE WRIGHT PLANNED their attempt to BECOME the FIRST men to FLY in an ENGINE-POWERED AIRPLANE.
_____ _____
What did Wilbur and Orville plan to do?

2.
Initiating event
When the two men AROSE at DAWN, the WIND was BRISK and a THREAT of RAIN lingered in the air
_____ _____
What was the weather like the day of the flight?

3.
Elaboration (description)
The DECISION they had to make was DIFFICULT. It might be DANGEROUS to fly in high WINDS, especially IF they ENCOUNTERED a SUDDEN GUST. But if the WIND held steady, it COULD actually HELP them in TAKING OFF.
_____ _____
Why was their decision difficult?

Reaction
WILBUR and ORVILLE were NERVOUS as they made their historic decision.

4.
Attempt
At about NOON, they STARTED the ENGINE. Suspense mounted as the AIRPLANE MOVED forward and gradually LIFTED into the air.
_____ _____
What happened about noon that day?

5.
Outcome
The machine FLEW for a brief TWELVE SEC ONDS before COMING to a HALT on the ground.
_____ _____
How did the flight turn out? How long did they fly?

6.
Resolution
Wilbur and Orville were TRIUMPHANT. They had accomplished their goal. Their achievement that day marked the BEGINNING of man's VENTURE INTO the SKY.
_____ _____
Why was their achievement important?

Listening
Comprehension/Nar F2

1. A CATERPILLAR makes a sleeping bag called a COCOON. It USES a kind of STICKY THREAD that comes from its mouth.

    _____ _____

    What is the cocoon made of?

2. First the caterpillar GRABS a TWIG with its BACK FEET. This leaves the front part of its body free to move.

    _____ _____

    What is first thing the caterpillar does? (How does it grab the twig?)

3. Then it begins to BEND and TURN and SPIN the THREAD around itself and the twig like a net. But it leaves room inside the net to move around.

    _____ _____

    What does the caterpillar do after it grabs the twig?

4. When the net is made the caterpillar MOVES its HEAD back and forth to PUT in a FLOOR.

    _____ _____

    What happens after the net is made?

5. Then it FILLS in all the SPACES in the net and finally CLOSES it all up.

    _____ _____

    What does it do after it puts in the floor?

6. After that the caterpillar goes to SLEEP. When it WAKES up in a few months it will be a MOTH.

    _____ _____

    What happens after the net is finally closed?

Listening
Comprehension/Exp F2

		Response		
		<u>Retell</u>	<u>Probe</u>	<u>Probe</u> <u>Questions</u>

1. You can still FIND GOLD in some California streams. All you NEED is a METAL PAN and a lot of LUCK.

    _____ _____

    What do you need to pan for gold?

2. First SELECT a place where the CURRENT is SLOW. GOLD is CARRIED BY moving WATER, but DROPS to the stream bed WHERE the WATER is STILL.

    _____ _____

    What is the first thing you should do? (Why is it best to pan where the water is still?)

3. Next SCOOP some GRAVEL from the stream INTO your PAN and gently WASH OUT and DIRT.

    _____ _____

    What is the first thing you do with your scoop of gravel?

4. Then PUT a little WATER in the PAN and ROCK it in a circle so that the larger bits of GRAVEL will SPILL OUT.

    _____ _____

    What do you do when the dirt is washed out?

5. Soon there should be only a HANDFUL of SAND LEFT. LOOK for SHINY YELLOW PARTICLES.

    _____ _____

    What is left when the gravel spills out of the pan?

6. You can DETERMINE if these are GOLD by HITTING them WITH a HAMMER. Real GOLD will FLATTEN BECAUSE it is SOFT.

    _____ _____

    How can you tell if the shiny particles are gold?

Silent Reading
Comprehension/Exp F1

		Retell	Probe	
Setting	Hundreds of RACERS were SET at the starting line.			
1. Elaboration	The most POPULAR BICYCLE RACE in the world was about to begin. It is called the TOUR DE FRANCE.	_____	_____	What is the Tour de France?
2. Initiating event	As the starting gun sounded, the RACERS SET OUT on a GRUELING and DANGEROUS COURSE. For 24 DAYS they would race over 2500 MILES	_____	_____	Describe the course How long is the race?
3. Elaboration	of French countryside, through BUSY CITY STREETS and over RUGGED mountain ROADS.	_____	_____	Where does the course go?
Reaction	For the first few miles RACERS were TENSE but EXCITED.			
4. Elaboration	The CROWDS which lined every small town and village along the route CHEERED encouragement.	_____	_____	What were the first few miles like?
5. Attempt	Several days into the race a FEW cyclists had BROKEN away from the PACK. Each in turn CHALLENGED for the LEAD as they headed UP a steep MOUNTAIN pass.	_____	_____	What happened several days into the race? Who challenged for the lead?
6. Elaboration	DETERMINATION, SKILL, and LUCK became critical FACTORS.	_____	_____	What were the critical factors in getting the lead?
7. Outcome	SOME QUIT when they became too TIRED to keep pedaling up the mountain. OTHERS lost control on the way down the other side, SKIDDING OFF the ROAD and slamming into rocky ditches at speeds approaching 60 miles an hour. SEVERAL DROPPED OUT when their EQUIPMENT FAILED.	_____	_____	What events knocked some of the leaders out of the race?
8. Resolution	In the end THREE racers headed out, seemingly ALONE, across the level plains TOWARD a still distant FINISH line. Only ONE would WIN the MONEY and FAME that goes to the champion.	_____	_____	How did the story end?

Silent Reading
Comprehension/Nar G1

		Response		Probe
		Retell	Probe	Questions

The SEAHORSE is an ODD kind of FISH.

1. It is THREE INCHES tall and looks LIKE a MATCHSTICK frame COVERED with fine CLOTH. _____ _____ What does the seahorse look like? Describe it's body.

2. Its SKIN is BROWN, it has a SNOUT like a TUBE and has long HAIRS on its HEAD. _____ _____ Describe its head.

3. If you watched a seahorse you might notice that it SWIMS UPRIGHT, but spends most of the time with its TAIL HOOKED around SEAPLANTS. _____ _____ How does a seahorse swim? How does it spend its time?

4. Since these PLANTS are also BROWN, the SEAHORSE is often DIFFICULT to FIND. _____ _____ Why is a seahorse hard to find?

5. When it is hungry the seahorse EATS small WORMS and SHELLFISH which it SUCKS OFF PLANTS with its long SNOUT. _____ _____ What does a seahorse eat? How does it get its food?

6. When it is time to reproduce, the FEMALE LAYS EGGS LIKES all other FISH. _____ _____ When it is time to reproduce, what does the female do?

7. But it is the MALE that TAKES CARE of them. He BABYSITS the eggs by KEEPING them in a POUCH UNTIL they HATCH. _____ _____ What does the male do? How?

8. Thus, although the SEAHORSE is a FISH, the way it LOOKS, SWIMS, and HATCHES its EGGS makes it a very UNUSUAL fish, indeed! _____ _____ What makes the seahorse an unusual fish?

Silent Reading
Comprehension/Exp G1

INTERACTIVE READING ASSESSMENT SYSTEM

IRAS-R

Student Pages

Developed by

Robert C. Calfee
University of California, Riverside
Kathryn Hoover Calfee
Palo Alto Unified School District

a   s   m   u   e   n

c   p   l   o   t   d

Alphabet Recognition

A   S   M   U   E   N

C   P   L   O   T   D

Alphabet Recognition

X

mud

pig

its

glad

sent

top

Y

spent

rub

basket

until

them

fist

Decoding/Vocabulary

A

end

long

little

time

house

same

B

food

city

best

paper

tell

room

C

fast

black

feel

table

birds

cold

D

music

watch

explain

color

heat

machine

Decoding/Vocabulary

E

skin

race

afraid

please

fight

middle

F

hungry

finger

visit

electric

crowd

kitchen

G

lonely

development

ability

honor

observe

industry

H

committee

atom

delicate

judge

prevent

mission

Decoding/Vocabulary

I

issue

muscle

annual

curiosity

literature

permanent

J

decade

bomb

promptly

grease

demonstrate

extensive

K

deserve

retain

consequence

graduation

ominous

skyscraper

L

proclaim

elegance

controversial

astute

aroma

implement

Decoding/Vocabulary

M	**N**
pessimistic	mandatory
dormant	flamboyant
boredom	traverse
prudent	veritable
illuminate	anthology
frustration	tumultuous

Decoding/Vocabulary

List 1	List 2
hin	shile
nelp	throve
flass	snay
scrong	toin
pame	spawk
vute	spleek

Letter Sound Correspondence

List 3	List 4
clur	worch
derb	knop
folp	ceft
sark	flage
shald	wrudge
plair	glies

Letter Sound Correspondence

List 5	List 6
lod - ded	jemming
fen - ing	saped
wem - bick	rimple
lude - ful	befade
un - fro - ten	dacture
im - pen - tive	conspartable
af - fre - mi - a - tion	rhosmic
syn - thod	paraplast
an - a - phen - ist	euchormonium

Letter Sound Correspondence

A. I like to play.

   I like to eat a red apple.

B. Ann wants Mom to make a cake. Mom
   cannot do it. She has to go to work.

C. The man made the light shine. Right away Ed
   saw the baby fox on top of its cage.

D. The kitten was scared and climbed up the
   tree. The girl tried to reach it but she had no
   luck.

E. Jeff was afraid that he would miss the first act. As
   soon as he bought the popcorn, he hurried to find
   Rose.

F. About three miles from the harbor, Ray's boat was caught in an unexpected current. He spotted a tiny island and realized that he was approaching its shore.

G. Harriet made many heroic attempts to lead other slaves to freedom in the North. Her courage and determination made her an important figure in the nation's history.

H. Slowly the women ascended the steep and icy mountain. There were times when the sheer cliffs and the bitter cold discouraged them, but they would not relent.

It is a sunny day. Ann is on her bike.

Tom wants to play ball. He asks Ann to

play with him. She will not play ball

now, she wants to ride.

Tom is sad. He asks Ann, "Can we take

a ride and then play ball?"

"Yes," says Ann. "That will be fun."

So Tom gets his bike and they play.

Oral Reading
Comprehensive/Nar Al

Jill has a tree house. She wants to paint it green.

She asks Sam to help.

Sam cannot help. He is going out with Pat.

Jill is sad. She asks Dad, "Can you come out and help me?"

"Yes," says Dad. "I will help you tree house."

So Jill goes to get the green paint.

Listening
Comprehension/Nar A2

Pam lived in a house by a hill.

One morning she took her brown ball to the top of the hill.

The grass was wet and Pam fell. The ball rolled down the hill.

Pam began to cry. She ran after it, but she could not stop it.

She saw it fall into a pond.

Then a boy walked by the pond. He saw something in the water.

Pam said, "Try to get my ball."

The boy jumped into the cold water. He got Pam's ball.

Pam thanked him and then walked up the hill and played.

Oral Reading
Comprehension/Nar B1

You should see Ann's dog. His name is Ed. He is bigger than Ann. She thinks he is getting bigger and bigger all the time.

His coat is red, but the hair on his head is dark brown. He has long thin legs and big fat feet. He has a big nose, too.

Ann thinks he is funny. He can run like a rabbit, but he eats like a pig.

Oral Reading
Comprehension/Exp B1

Ed works at the zoo in town. One night he took some food to the baby fox. He went to its cage, but the fox was not there.

Ed was surprised. He looked around, but he did not see it. The fox hid in the dark.

Then a man walked by. He had a light. Ed said, "Shine the light on the cage." The man made the light shine.

Right away Ed saw the baby fox on top of its cage. So he put it back in the cage and gave it some food.

Listening
Comprehension/Nar B2

Bill was dressed for winter. He had on a round, fur hat. It was pulled down over his ears. His long coat was buttoned up to his chin. The buttons were big and red. They made him look like a clown.

Yes, Bill was dressed for the cold. He had on his fur hat and his long coat. I laughed when he hopped up and down to keep his feet warm.

Listening
Comprehension/Exp B2

Once there was an old man who lived by a river. It was winter and the river was covered with ice. One day he looked out his window and saw a boy by the river. The boy started to walk across the river on the ice.

The old man was afraid that the ice would break. He opened the window and called out to the boy. But the boy didn't hear him, and he just kept on going. When he got to the middle, the ice broke, and the boy fell into the water.

The old man got a long ladder and ran down to the river. He slid the ladder across the ice. The boy grabbed the ladder and the man pulled him out.

The next day the boy visited the old man and thanked him for saving his life.

Oral Reading
Comprehension/Nar C1

It is easy to make butter. First you need a jar and some heavy cream. Fill the jar part way with cream. Then shake it for about 20 minutes. Soon the cream will start to get lumpy. Stop when most of the cream turns into lumps. You will find that the lumps are butter.

Take the lumps out of the jar and wash them with cold water. Mix a little salt with the lumps and pat them together. Leave the butter in a cool place over night. In the morning the butter will be hard and ready to eat.

Oral Reading
Comprehension/Exp C1

Once there was a little girl who had a kitten. The kitten liked to play in the yard by a tall tree.

Early one morning a dog was walking in front of the house. It was windy and the gate blew open. The dog ran into the yard. The kitten was scared and ran up the tree.

The girl tried to reach it, but she had no luck. The kitten climbed to the highest branch. The girl's sister saw the kitten from her window. She opened the window and leaned out. She could reach the branch. "Come inside," she said softly. She reached out when the kitten came closer. Then she pulled it into the house.

That night the little girl told everyone what had happened. She was glad that her sister had saved the kitten.

Listening
Comprehension/Nar C2

One way to make money in the summer is to sell lemonade. It is easy to make. You need lemons, water, sugar, and ice.

Put the juice from ten lemons into ten cups of water. Add two cups of sugar and lots of ice. Then stir it.

When you have the lemonade, get some paper cups and enough money to make change. Also get a small table to put things on. Then find a spot to set up. The corner of a street is good.

When it gets hot, people will stop to buy a drink.

Listening
Comprehension/Exp C2

Joe and his daughter Sue were fishing at the lake. They were there for an hour and had not caught any fish.

Joe wanted to find a better spot so he started to walk around the lake. He passed a few fishermen near the dock. They told him that they were catching lots of fish.

Joe was excited to hear the news, and he started back to get his daughter.

Meanwhile, Sue was fishing by herself. She got tired and fell asleep with the pole in her hand. She slept until she felt a strong tug on her line. She was startled to find that the fishing rod was being pulled into the water.

Sue rushed into the lake just as her father returned. Then she grabbed the fishing pole and pulled it out of the water.

Both Joe and Sue were amazed to discover an enormous fish hooked on the line.

Oral Reading
Comprehension/Nar D1

There is a big, old tree in the yard outside my window. It is straight and tall and looks like a cone. The branches at the bottom are wide and full. The tree goes way above the roof of my house. At the top it is narrow and comes to a point. The green leaves that cover its branches are not really leaves at all. They are sharp and pointed and make me think of needles.

The tree in my yard is always green. In winter the other trees lose their leaves. But even when snow falls and it is cold I can look at my tree and think of spring.

Oral Reading
Comprehension/Exp D1

Kate and her cousin, Jeff, went to the circus. They arrived a half-hour before the afternoon show.

Kate wanted to find good seats. She walked inside and saw two empty seats in the first row, but a lady told her that the seats were taken. Kate was unhappy because the front rows were already filled. She walked to the back to find two seats.

Meanwhile, Jeff was waiting in line at the candy stand. He wanted to get some popcorn before the show began. Suddenly he heard the band begin to play. He was afraid that he would miss the first act. As soon as he bought the popcorn, he hurried to find Kate. On the way to his seat, he tripped and spilled the popcorn.

Finally, he found his cousin in the back row and they began to watch the show. They didn't have good seats and they didn't have any popcorn, but they enjoyed the circus anyway.

Listening
Comprehension/Nar D2

Not far from where I live there is an old castle. It is not very big. It is made of gray stones and has a tower on one side of the main building. The tower is round and about 30 feet tall. There is a long narrow window near the top. The glass in the window has been broken for many years.

There is a cellar hole on the other side of the castle. It is filled with rocks and weeds. Some wood also remains from the barn that used to be there.

It is easy to tell that no one has lived there for a long time. Even the road is grown over with grass.

Listening
Comprehension/Exp D2

The moon had just risen as Jan looked toward the old deserted house. She was waiting for her friend, Ellen. Together they planned to find out if the house was haunted.

When Ellen arrived the two friends began to walk nervously up the path. A strange shadow seemed to fall across the window next to the porch. Both girls were scared, but they pretended not to notice. Then as Ellen held the flashlight, Jan anxiously pushed open the door.

Once inside the house they were startled to hear a peculiar scratching sound. Ellen flashed her light all around, but she could not find where the sound was coming from. But it seemed to be coming toward them.

Suddenly Jan felt something rub against her leg. She tried to scream but was too scared to make a sound. She grabbed Ellen's arm and stared at her in shock.

Ellen flashed the light her way, and then they both realized what was haunting the house. It was just an old black cat who had made the house its home.

Silent Reading
Comprehension/Nar E1

An amusement park is opening in town next Saturday. There will be a parade, fireworks, and free admission on opening day. More than five thousand people are expected to attend.

Work first began on the park two years ago. At that time the site was an unused field. It was filled with weeds and trash. Although occasional attempts had been made to clean it up, nothing had worked. Since then, more than fifty rides, a playhouse, and a picnic ground have been built. Many trees and bushes also have been planted.

After opening day, admission to the park will cost three dollars. However, children under twelve will be let in free if they come with an adult. All rides will cost fifty cents, except the rollercoaster, which will cost a dollar.

Silent Reading
Comprehension/Exp E1

It was late afternoon. Alice stood by the open barn door. She had latched the door this morning, but now it was open and her horse, Sam, was missing. Alice feared that Sam would not return before nightfall. So she decided to go look for him.

A short way from the barn she spotted Sam grazing in a pasture, but he was not alone. Another horse from a neighbor's farm was alongside him. Alice was surprised to see the other horse.

She got two ropes and went into the pasture after the horses. When she finally caught both of them, Alice put Sam back in the barn. Then she tried to tie the other horse to a nearby post, but be broke loose from her grasp. Alice was beginning to get angry. She tried to catch the horse again, but before she could reach him, he ran to the barn and lifted the latch with his nose.

Suddenly Alice realized why the door had been open. The neighbor's horse had let Sam out.

Listening
Comprehension/Nar E2

A group of students is planning to start a nature club. Anyone interested in wild animals, birds, plants, or wilderness biking is invited to join. No membership fee will be charged.

The club is being formed in order to combine the interests of several smaller groups. In the past these groups have not had enough members to become official school clubs. At least twenty members are needed to meet school requirements.

There are several benefits to having an official club. The school provides an adult advisor, money for activities, and help in planning field trips. It also provides office space and allows the club to hold meetings during school hours. Without these benefits it is difficult for groups to function.

Listening
Comprehension/Exp E2

It was the year 1849 in the small town of Buckstown, Maryland. A young, black slave, named Harriet Tubman, decided to escape from the South and seek her freedom. Harriet awaited a chance to begin the trip northward.

One evening a farmer volunteered to hide Harriet in his cart underneath a load of vegetables. Harriet was terrified that she would be caught trying to escape, but she was determined to take the risk.

Harriet traveled on a route known as the underground railroad. The underground was not a real railroad, but an organization of people who provided rides and hiding places for slaves escaping from plantations in the South.

Harriet spent several exhausting nights traveling. Finally she arrived at the Pennsylvania border. She was a free citizen for the first time in her life.

Afterward, Harriet made many heroic attempts to lead other slaves to freedom in the North. Because of her courage and determination she is an important figure in the nation's history.

Silent Reading
Comprehension/Nar F1

You can still find gold in some California streams. All you need is a metal pan and a lot of luck.

First select a place where the current is slow. Gold is carried by moving water, but drops to the stream bed where the water is still. Next scoop some gravel from the stream into your pan and gently wash out any dirt. Then put a little water in the pan and rock it in a circle so that the larger bits of gravel will spill out. Soon there should be only a handful of sand left. Look for shiny yellow particles. You can determine if these are gold by hitting them with a hammer. Real gold will flatten because it is soft.

Silent Reading
Comprehension/Exp F1

It was winter in the town of Kitty Hawk, North Carolina. This was the day Wilbur and Orville Wright planned an attempt to become the first men to fly in an engine-powered airplane.

When the two men arose at dawn the wind was brisk and a threat of rain lingered in the air. The decision they had to make was difficult. It might be dangerous to fly in high winds, especially if there were a sudden gust. But if the wind held steady it could actually help them in taking off. Wilbur and Orville were nervous as they made the historic decision.

At about noon, they started the engine. Suspense mounted as the airplane moved forward and gradually lifted into the air. The machine flew for a brief twelve seconds before coming to a halt on the ground.

Wilbur and Orville were triumphant. They had accomplished their goal. Their achievement that day marked the beginning of man's venture into the sky.

Listening
Comprehension/Nar F2

A caterpillar makes a sleeping bag called a cocoon. It uses a kind of sticky thread that comes from its mouth.

First the caterpillar grabs a twig with its back feet. This leaves the front part of its body free to move. Then it begins to bend and turn and spin the thread around itself and the twig like a net. But it leaves room inside the net to move around.

When the net is made, the caterpillar moves its head back and forth to put in a floor. Then it fills in all the spaces in the net and finally closes it all up.

After that, the caterpillar goes to sleep. When it wakes up in a few months, it will be a moth.

Listening
Comprehension/Exp F2

Hundreds of racers were set at the starting line. The most popular bicycle race in the world was about to begin. It is called the Tour de France.

As the starting gun sounded, the racers set out on a grueling and dangerous course. For 24 days they would race over 2500 miles of French countryside, through busy city streets and over rugged mountain roads.

For the first few miles racers were tense but excited. The crowds which lined every small town and village along the route cheered encouragement. Several days into the race a few cyclists had broken away from the pack. Each in turn challenged for the lead as they headed up a steep mountain pass. Determination, skill, and luck became critical factors.

Some quit when they became too tired to keep peddling up the mountain. Others lost control on the way down the other side, skidding off the road and slamming into rocky ditches at speeds approaching 60 miles an hour. Several dropped out when their equipment failed.

In the end three racers headed out, seemingly alone, across the level plains toward a still distant finish line. Only one would win the money and fame that goes to the champion.

Silent Reading
Comprehension/Nar G1

The seahorse is an odd kind of fish. It is three inches tall and looks like a matchstick frame covered with fine cloth. Its skin is brown, it has a snout like a tube, and has long hairs on its head.

If you watched a seahorse you might notice that it swims upright but spends most of the time with its tail hooked around seaplants. Since these plants are also brown, the seahorse if often difficult to find.

When it is hungry the seahorse eats small worms and shellfish which it sucks off plants with its long snout.

When it is time to reproduce, the female lays eggs like all other fish. But it is the male that takes care of them. He babysits the eggs by keeping them in a pouch until they hatch.

Thus, although the seahorse is a fish, the way it looks, swims, and hatches its eggs makes it a very unusual fish, indeed!

Silent Reading
Comprehension/Exp G1

Read-Write Cycle Assessments

Introduction

The Read-Write Cycle Assessments are dynamic assessments designed to determine the best writing a student can do on a given topic. The format used with this assessment is grounded in the tenets of social cognitive learning, closely resembles regular classroom instruction, and reflects the reading-writing connection. Included in the design are pre-writing activities that use cooperative/collaborative instructional strategies to scaffold each student's background knowledge. During the pre-writing activities, students work individually, in pairs or small groups, or as a whole class to pool their knowledge and understanding of the topic. These activities work to 'level the playing field' so that the students are better able to demonstrate their ability to compose text in an academic setting without being hampered by less than adequate topic knowledge. Teachers can get a clearer understanding of their students' skill in expressing ideas coherently and with organization, using appropriate vocabulary, grammar, and mechanics than they would when administering the more commonly utilized on-demand writing assessments.

The example assessment below is appropriate for upper elementary and middle school students. Ideally, it would be administered over a two-day block during one class period each day. A rubric for scoring the writing done on the second day is given after the assessment. Finally, an example of a Read-Write portfolio generated by a different Read-Write Cycle Assessment is given to illustrate the thought processes a student uses throughout the experience.

Once the teacher has become familiarized with the general design of a Read-Write Cycle assessment, he or she is encouraged to create their own versions to assess writing across the curriculum.

READ-WRITE CYCLE ASSESSMENT
ELEMENTARY & MIDDLE SCHOOL LEVEL
Winning the Lottery

Day 1 of 2

Topic: What would happen if my family (or I) won the Lottery?
Group Organization: Whole class or partners
Teacher Materials: Chart Paper, markers
Student Materials: Text, Group task sheets
Time: One class session, two days in a row

Note: Adjust the dialogue as appropriate for you and your students.

Pre-Reading: Introduce the activity. This segment should take 5-7 minutes.

<u>Connect</u>:   **"What would happen if your family (or you) won the lottery?"**
[Option: individual quick write, partner brainstorm]

<u>Brainstorm</u>:   **"Let's get some of your ideas on the chart paper. What would happen if your family (or you) won the lottery?"**

Prompts: **"What are some positive things?"**
                   "You've mentioned positives to having money. Any   negatives?"

Prompt students with questions regarding:
- behaviors
- emotions
- relationships
- other

Vocabulary to highlight: millionaire, purchase, opinion
[Check and adjust text to meet your students' needs.]

<u>Organize</u>:   **"Look at our brainstorming list. How might we group some of these ideas together? Let's think of some headings we could use to categorize the items we have on the list. We are going to organize the list by making a web. The web will help us think about our ideas. Now tell me where each item should go and why you think that is the best place for it."**

[Make a web with 'Winning the Lottery' in the center circle. Draw lines to circles surrounding the center circle, placing category titles in the surrounding circles. Place lines radiating out from the category title circles and write the appropriate items from the brainstorm list at the ends of the lines. Be sure to have the student justify the placement.]

[Students can make their own webs modeled on the class web.]

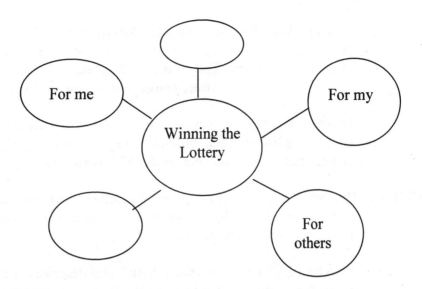

Purpose: **"During the next two days you will be talking and reading about what happens to people when they win large amounts of money – positive things and perhaps negative things. You will share your ideas and hear the ideas of others. Tomorrow you will write about how life would be different if you won the lottery. I will be looking at your writing to see the ways that you share your ideas on paper and to find what you like to write about. Later in the year, we will look at this piece of writing to see how you've developed as writers."**

Connect: [Lead into the text….]

Reading: Distribute the text. Students can read independently or with a partner.
[Note any additional support provided, i.e., teacher reading to a specific student.]
"As you read, think about the two questions on the side. Write down some notes either while you are reading or when you are finished." Plan about 5-7 minutes for reading and 5-7 minutes for individual responses to the passage.

Facilitate by drawing attention to the question and providing support/clarification as appropriate. [Since students read at various paces, have a plan for what they will do when finished.]

[Option: Whole-group discussion of student responses to questions.]

Post-Reading: Help students get started by introducing the activity as a whole-class discussion. Recreate the Venn diagram [see Group Task] on chart paper or overhead transparency. Explain the meaning of each section of the diagram {characteristics of having much money, little money, and commonalities.]

Organize: **"What is life like when you have lots of money?"**
    *Once students begin generating ideas, move into smaller groups [see below].
    Discussion prompts: **Tell us more about that.**
                                           Make connections between the sections.

    Divide students into groups of 2 or 4. Have them continue comparing and contrasting life with and without money. [Use your judgment for effective arrangements based on your students' experiences with cooperative groups.]

Small Group Report: The purposes are (a) to add further ideas and vocabulary to the original webbing chart, and (b) focus individual students on the theme or position for the upcoming writing assignment.

    "I'd like each group to share their Venn diagram. Tell us two or three of your items and where you put your items. If you hear something that you didn't think about for your Venn diagram, you can add it to yours."

    Each group will have 1-2 minutes to share highlights from their Venn diagrams.

Closure: Re-cap by adding new information to the web [as appropriate].
    "Tomorrow you will take this information, as well as the ideas you've heard from your classmates, and write about what your life would be like if you and your family won the lottery."

The dress is the lightest shade of blue: floor-length, fitted on top and flowing into a full skirt. It costs $139. For 15-year-old Cheyanne Maples, owning this dress would have been impossible in the past.

Today Cheyanne and her brother, John, don't even look at price tags as they shop for the big dance.

Three months ago, their mother, who worked at a company for 25 years, lost her job because the plant was shut down.

But the family got lucky! Just after losing the job, they became millionaires by winning the Lotto. The prize was beyond their wildest dreams! For the next 20 years, their mother will receive $135,000.

Shop till you drop

That money has meant changes for the family. The Maples purchased a satellite dish, a new dishwasher, and two new cars (one a Miata). They are planning to build a new house. Everyone is wearing new clothes.

The family agrees that shopping is the best part of winning the lottery.

Talk of the halls

At West Lake High School, where Cheyanne and John go to school, news of the big win spread fast. Everybody knew about their good luck – and everybody had an opinion about it.

On the first day, Cheyanne received a marriage proposal in the cafeteria ("He was on his knees right in front of my lunch tray!" she groans.)

Soon life got back to normal. Cheyanne still spends one class period working in the school office; John still stays after school to play chess.

It looks the same from the outside, but some things have changed. Cheyanne's friend Annie thinks the money's made Cheyanne forget her real friends. "I'm glad it wasn't me," she says, "money makes people do stupid things."

And Jason says, "John got a big head. All he talks about is what he's bought and what he's going to by next."

Cheyanne thinks people notice her more now. She asks, "Why didn't they like me before? It's not like I have any more money. My Mom does."

They also know that while money can change what you have, it cannot change who you are or what your parents expect from you. In the end, it's their money.

John might be able to buy expensive clothes, but he still gets in trouble for not putting his clothes in the dryer.

The bottom line?

Money can bring you wonderful things, but you'll still be the same person you always were, coping with the same stuff you always did.

What do you think about how the family decided to spend their money?

They got their money three months ago. What so you think their lives will be like in a yea

READ-WRITE CYCLE ASSESSMENT
ELEMENTARY & MIDDLE SCHOOL LEVEL
Winning the Lottery

Day 2 of 2

Topic:	What would happen if I won the Lottery?
Group Organization:	Whole class & individuals
Teacher Materials:	Chart Paper, markers
Student Materials:	Pre-writing worksheet, writing paper, previous day's materials
Time:	One class session, two days in a row

Note: Adjust the dialogue as appropriate for you and your students.

Pre-Writing: Whole-class activity. Review the previous day's session, remind students of topic, webbing chart, and Venn diagram. Hand out the Pre-Writing Worksheet and instruct students about how to transfer key words from the webbing chart, and how to add their own words to the worksheet. You may also direct the students to include a graphic organizer [e.g., matrix, re-organized web, Venn diagram] as part of their planning. This segment should take about 5-6 minutes.

Writing: Individual task. The students will have access to the Pre-Writing Worksheet and the Webbing Chart (Day 1), and other resources allowed by the teacher, including dictionary and thesaurus. Discuss and ask questions about the directions for the writing task to ensure that all the students understand what they are being asked to do. Remember, the goal is to obtain optimal performance. Students may ask the teacher for clarification about the task, but students may not help one another. This segment should take 12-15 minutes.

Post-Writing: Whole-class activity. Debrief class after the papers are turned in. **"How did you feel about the writing task?"** [words of advice, problems]. Students can briefly assess their performance [think to self, talk with a neighbor, provide an appropriate signal]. This segment should take 2-5 minutes.

Group Task: Venn Diagram   **Name** _____   **Name** _____

List 5 – 7 items in each section.

Having a Million Dollars   **Having Little Money**

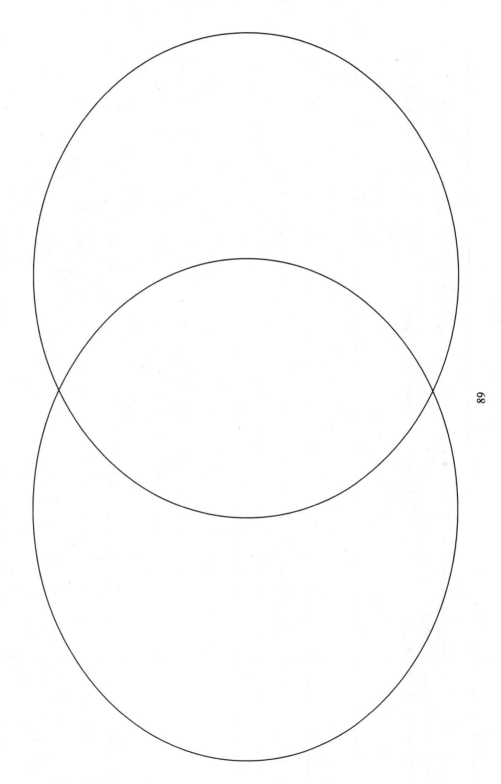

89

Pre-Writing Worksheet   Name _____   Date _____

List 5 – 7 items for each question. Find words from the web and the Venn diagram that will help you when you write.
Use words, phrases, pictures, or sentences.

What would I do for <u>myself</u>?	What would my family do for <u>each other</u>?	What would my family and I do for <u>others</u>? [friends, neighbors, our community, strangers, etc.]

Winning the Lottery   **Name** _____ **Date** _____

Choose one topic. Write 1 – 2 pages about you and your family winning the lottery. Use your Pre-Writing Worksheets to get ideas and words for your paper. You can also use new ideas.

When you finish, read your paper again.
- Will the reader understand what you are thinking?
- Check for spelling. and grammar (periods, capitals, etc.)

1.   **If my family and I won the lottery,...**

or

2.   **I think that my family and I should win the lottery because...**

_____

_____

_____

_____

_____

_____

_____

_____

_____

_____

_____

_____

_____

_____

_____

_____

_____

_____

Figure: Read-Write Cycle Assessment Rubric

Score	Length*	Coherence	Grammar / Mechanics
6	3 - 5 pages or 176 or more words	• **Writer provides overall links / transitions; examples and descriptions are presented logically.** • States main topic and supports with details and examples • Shifts topics easy to follow and logical	• Few, if any, errors in grammar and punctuation • **Utilizes appropriate variety of sentence structures, including phrases and clauses**
5	1-2 pages or 86-175 words	• **Ease and facility in expressing ideas** • Writing flows smoothly and naturally, and is understandable • Generally focused on topic • Provides description, elaboration, evidence, and/or support • **Writer provides overall links,** but transitions may not always be smooth; **ideas/reasons are clear and logical**	• **Some variation in sentence structure, including phrases and clauses** • Minimal errors may be present as students explore complex structures. • Few run-ons or fragmented sentences
4	3/4 page or 61-85 words	• **Provides descriptions, elaboration, evidence and/or support** • Information or examples may be in a list-like form (no tying together of ideas) • Addresses the topic without wavering • Writing is generally understandable and coherent, but lacks complete control • Focus may shift and be somewhat difficult to follow.	• **Clear sentence sense** • May display variety in sentences • **Minimal or no errors in punctuation** • Few, if any, run-ons or fragmented sentences
3	4 sentences/ 1/2 page or 36-60 words	• **Addresses the topic** • **little description, elaboration, evidence or support** • May construct rambling sentences or lists with no elaboration • Vague and/or confusing	• **Simple repetitive sentences** • May include fragments and run-ons • Some errors in punctuation and grammar which do not impede reading
2	2 - 3 sentences/ 1/4 page or 11-35 words	• **Addresses the topic minimally** • May wander off topic • Fragmented expression of ideas	• **Simple sentence structure or phrases with many fragments and/or run-ons** • **Errors are highly evident and interfere with reading**
1	1 sentence or less or 0-10 words	• **Generally unintelligible or unrelated** • **Copied** from the board or another student	• **Unintelligible due to grammar or punctuation** • **Copied** from the board or another student

*Grade-level appropriate paper, margins, and penmanship; no skipping lines

Figure: Read-Write Cycle Assessment Rubric cont.

Score	Vocabulary	Spelling
6	<ul><li>**Substantial use of complex Romance words**</li><li>**Lexical variety**</li><li>precision in dealing with topic.</li><li>**Latin and Greek roots and affixes**</li></ul>	**Complex Conventional**<ul><li>**Substantial evidence of attempting complex words with few errors** (polysyllabic words, prefixes and suffixes, Latin & Greek roots & affixes</li><li>Command of vowels in polysyllabic words</li><li>**Mastery of conventional spellings for familiar 1-2 syllable words**</li></ul>
5	<ul><li>Some evidence of **complex but familiar Romance words**</li><li>Limited variety and reliance on relatively common words (national).</li><li>**Latin (& Greek) roots and affixes**</li><li>**Precise and/or rich language** (No ordinary friend, compassionate)</li></ul>	**Conventional**<ul><li>**Command of long/short vowel contrast**</li><li>**Few errors**</li><li>Polysyllabic words are present and have few or no errors</li></ul>
4	<ul><li>Substantial number of familiar polysyllabic words (interesting, understand) including compounds</li><li>**Noticeable increased precision** ('friendly' for 'nice').</li></ul>	**Phonetic Appropriate**<ul><li>**Beginning to show long/short vowel contrast**</li><li>Short vowels accurate</li><li>**May have other vowel errors** (e.g. digraphs)</li><li>Reversals may be present (especially in blends and r/l patterns</li><li>Polysyllabic words (including compounds), if present, include vowels</li></ul>
3	<ul><li>**1 - 2 syllable words**, but mostly frequent and little variety or precision</li><li>May include compounds and *Anglo-Saxon affixation (propositions, comparatives: under-, -er, -est)</li><li>May include descriptive words</li></ul>	**Phonological**<ul><li>**Short vowels accurate**</li><li>**Represents each sound (except)—very few omissions**</li><li>Reversals may be present (especially in blends or r/l patterns</li><li>**Easily readable**</li></ul>
2	<ul><li>**Frequent one-syllable (CVC) and basic sight words**</li><li>Short "safe" words, commonplace</li><li>Simplistic and/or imprecise language</li></ul>	**Beginning Phonological**<ul><li>**Identification of consonants**</li><li>Vowels are included, but frequently incorrect selection</li><li>Omission of sounds (sitr=sister)</li><li>**Readable with minimal effort**</li></ul>
1	<ul><li>**Most words difficult to interpret**</li><li>Few words and/or limited to words provided by the teacher</li><li>Incorrect and/or ineffective language use</li></ul>	**Alphabetic, Pre-Phonetic**<ul><li>Uses letters</li><li>Consonants may represent some sounds</li><li>Omission of most vowels</li><li>Sight words may or may not be spelled conventionally</li><li>**Unreadable or readable with considerable effort**</li></ul>

*Most Anglo-Saxon words can stand alone and be affixed. Affixes are often prepositional: over-, under-, in-, for-. Common suffixes include: -ed, -er, -ing, -ly, -hood, -ness

The Read-Write Cycle: Portfolio Entries from a Fifth-Grade Student

The following series of portfolio entries illustrate a fifth-grader's efforts as she and her classmates work on a read-write cycle task. Portfolio entries, such as those that follow, can help the teacher understand the thinking processes their students use as they work through a read-write cycle assessment. The teacher can also use the data gathered to inform future writing instruction. By comparing the prewriting graphic organizers, the writing sample, and the portfolio entries from a series of read-write cycle assessments at the beginning, middle, and end of the school year, it is possible for teachers, students, and the students' parents to gain a clear picture of the students' growth in writing skills across the academic year.

DEVELOP: The big problem for us fifth-graders is that our school has decided to replace all the desserts in the cafeteria with fruit. We think that we should have a choice of fruit or a dessert. When we talked to our teacher about it, she suggested that we write a letter to the principal and the school board about this decision. We brainstormed what things we might put in our letter. Our teacher even brought in an article from the newspaper for all of us to read. It was about how the Los Angeles Unified School District has decided to cut back on sugar available in their schools. They are replacing their high-sugar desserts with different kinds of fruit. We even went to the library and the Internet to find out more about how much sugar is in different fruits and desserts. We were able to add to our brainstorm and then organized all of that information into a matrix, so we could think about it better.

[Portfolio includes brainstorming results]

DRAFT: Fifth-graders are old enough to make good choices about their health. The school really needs to offer a selection of foods that we could eat as a dessert. We made a list of desserts and fruit so we can compare the sugar in them. Our class would like to meet with you to talk about possible choices that the cafeteria could have for us.

[This is a synposis of a two-page draft, all of which is included in the portfolio.]

REVIEW: I asked other students about the letter, and they suggested a couple of things. One was to find out how much each dessert choice would cost. Another was that it will take a while to do anything. Are we expecting changes before we go on to middle school?

[Evidence that the student has consulted with peers and learned something from the experience.]

REVISE: Some of us have talked with our parents, and they are willing to help. Three of them have written letters promising to meet with you and with our group. We also know that changing the cafeteria menu will take a while. It's May, and we will soon be leaving for middle school. But we think that a choice of foods will be good for everyone, and so we are willing to help solve the

94

dessert problem even if it won't make things better for us.
[This is one of several notes on revising that are in the portfolio.]

POLISH: We looked over the revision for spelling and grammar errors and other ways to improve the final version.

[The portfolio contains several drafts, making it possible to see how successful students were in revising.]

PUBLISH
[The letter, prepared on a computer and signed by all of the students, was delivered to the principal's office by a delegation. The portfolio includes a photograph of the principal receiving the letter from the students.]

Dear Ms. S,
Our fifth-grade class is worried about the changes in cafeteria food available at our school. We all have different likes and dislikes. We enjoy having the opportunity to choose from a variety of foods. We also like it better when we know if the food we eat is good for us or not.

Having a larger choice of desserts will cost more money for the school. We did some research about the amount of sugar in different kinds of desserts and fruits. We made a list of the foods that had the lowest amount of sugar to help you compare the sugar content and the number of calories. We also estimated how much a serving of each fruit or dessert would cost.

We have talked with our parents, and three of them have promised to meet with you and us to talk about how to fix the food choice problem. It will take a while to make changes in the lunch menu, and since we are graduating in May, it won't help us. But delicious, healthy choices in the cafeteria will help everyone. We have talked with the fourth-graders, and they agree. Will you meet with our class and our parents to see what we can do?

Sincerely,
The 2005 Fifth-Grade Class

REPORT NOTES

Project READ Plus

This form can help the reader analyze the features of a report or exposition. It can also be used to plan for the writing of a research paper or summarizing a chapter.

MAIN TOPIC: Look over the title and skim the report headings and paragraphs. What is the article mostly about?

_____

_____

TYPE OF REPORT: Reports give information, explain a process, or argue a position. What is the purpose of this article?

_____

_____

INTRODUCTION/OVERVIEW: Read the first paragraph carefully. It should tell you what the article is going to do and why. If the first paragraph is really an introduction, write down the main points in this paragraph. Otherwise, tell what the paragraph does do.

_____

_____

SUMMARY: Sometimes the last paragraph goes through the main points. Skip to the end, read the last paragraph, and describe what you find there.

_____

_____

MAIN "CHUNKS:" Using what you have already written above, divide the article into no more than five "chunks," and summarize what happens in each of these in a sentence or two. Circle the KEY WORDS in each chunk.

#1_____

_____

#2_____

_____

#3_____

_____

#4_____

_____

#5_____

_____

SUMMARY: Now write your own summary of the article!

Introduction to the Lesson Plans

In this section of the booklet, we have included five lesson plans, illustrating several different sorts of instruction. Each lesson plan is related to a chapter in *Teaching Reading in the 21st Century* 4/E, and you can learn more about the sorts of instruction illustrated in each lesson plan by consulting the appropriate chapter in the book.

The first lesson plan is a detailed description of an in-depth procedure for teaching students to infer the meanings of unknown words they come across as they read. Teaching students to use context clues is both very important and something that takes a good deal of time and effort on your part and on the part of your students. As you go through this lesson, you will see that it is indeed a robust one. More information on teaching context clues can be found in Chapter 7: Vocabulary Development.

The second lesson plan is a detailed description of an in-depth procedure for teaching students to unlock the meanings of unknown words using their knowledge of prefixes. Teaching students to use prefixes to unlock the meanings of words they do not know is another important word-learning strategy, and it too requires in-depth instruction. A list of the most frequent prefixes, those that are most worthy of instruction, is included in Chapter 5: Word Recognition. More information on teaching students to use prefixes and information on teaching them to use other word parts is included in Chapter 7: Vocabulary Development.

The third lesson plan is a Scaffolded Reading Experience (SRE) for teaching Kate DiCamillos' awarding winning novel *Because of Winn-Dixie*. In addition to helping students learn strategies such as using context and using prefixes, it is important to help students read, understand, learn from, and enjoy the books and other materials they read for your class. SREs are research based, powerful, and flexible ways to do that. More information on SREs can be found in Chapter 8: Scaffolding Students' Comprehension of Text, and many additional SREs can be found at onlinereadingresources.com.

The fourth lesson plan is a description of the first two days of instruction designed to teach kindergarteners the comprehension strategy of using prior knowledge. Comprehension is of course the ultimate goal of reading, and it is important to give students experiences that build their skill at comprehending text beginning in the earliest grades and continuing throughout the higher grades. More information on comprehension strategies and how to teach them can be found in Chapter 9: Teaching Comprehension Strategies.

The fifth and final lesson plan is a fairly detailed description of Questioning the Author (QtA), a type of comprehension instruction developed by Isable Beck and Margaret McKeown. QtA is a whole group questioning and discussion strategy designed to help students clarify any misunderstandings they have and construct significant meaning for what they read. It is one of several procedures for assisting students in building rich and lasting understanding of important topics, something we discuss in Chapter 11, Fostering Higher-Order Thinking and Deep Understanding.

Teaching Students to Use Context Clues to Infer the Meanings of Unknown Words

Taken with modifications from

The Vocabulary Book

by

Michael F. Graves

Published in 2006 by Teachers College Press, the International Reading Association, and the National Council of Teachers of English, and reprinted with permission.

Using context clues to infer the meanings of unknown words is the first word-learning strategy to consider because it is the most important one. Most words are learned from context, and if we can increase students' proficiency in learning from context even a small amount, we will greatly increase the number of words they learn. It is therefore vital that we provide students with rich, robust, and effective instruction on using context clues. Providing such instruction takes a good deal of time and effort on the part of both teachers and students. The instruction outlined here takes place over ten 30-45 minute sessions. A sample schedule is shown in Figure 1. In what follows, I describe the first two days of instruction in some detail and then much more briefly describe the rest of the unit. The instruction is described as it would be presented to students in the upper elementary grades. With younger or older students, the language and examples would be adjusted accordingly.

Figure 1. Overview of a Unit on Context Clues

DAY 1	DAY 2.	DAY 3	DAY 4	DAY 5
Motivation and Introduction to using context to infer meaning using a videotape	Introduction to using context clues to infer word meanings and to the four-step strategy	Detailed instruction in the first 2 steps of the strategy: Play and Question, and Slow Advance	Detailed instruction in the second 2 steps of the strategy: Stop and Rewind, and Play and Question	Game in which students earn points for using the four-step strategy to infer word meanings
DAY 6	DAY 7	DAY 8	DAY 9	DAY 10
Review of using context clues and the four-step strategy Renaming of the four steps without the VCR terminology	Guided practice — and further instruction if necessary—in using the four-step process with teacher provided narrative texts.	Guided practice — and further instruction if necessary—in using the four-step process with teacher provided expository texts.	Guided practice — and further instruction if necessary—in using the four-step process with authentic texts currently being used in the class.	Review of using context clues and the four-step strategy Student-teacher planning on strategically using and learning more about context clues

Day 1—Introduction and Motivation

Because learning to use context clues is a demanding and challenging task, the teacher introduces the unit with a substantial motivational activity designed to both gain students' interest and enable them to relate the task of using context clues to infer word meanings to an activity they are familiar with—using a VCR.

She begins by telling students that over the next few weeks the class is going to be working on using context clues to figure out the meanings of unknown words they come across while reading. Using clues to figure out things they don't know, she tells them, is something they do all the time, something they're good at, and something that is fun. Then, she tells them that they'll begin their study of context clues by viewing a brief video showing a place they might know and that their job is to look for clues to what the place is.

Just before showing the video, the teacher passes out the Clue Web shown in Figure 2, puts a copy of the Clue Web on the overhead, and tells students that they will use the Clue Web today as they watch the video and over the next few weeks as they learn to use context clues. She goes on to tell them that they probably won't be able to answer all of these questions and should jot down brief answers, while trying to figure out as much as possible about the place described in the video.

Figure 2. Clue Web

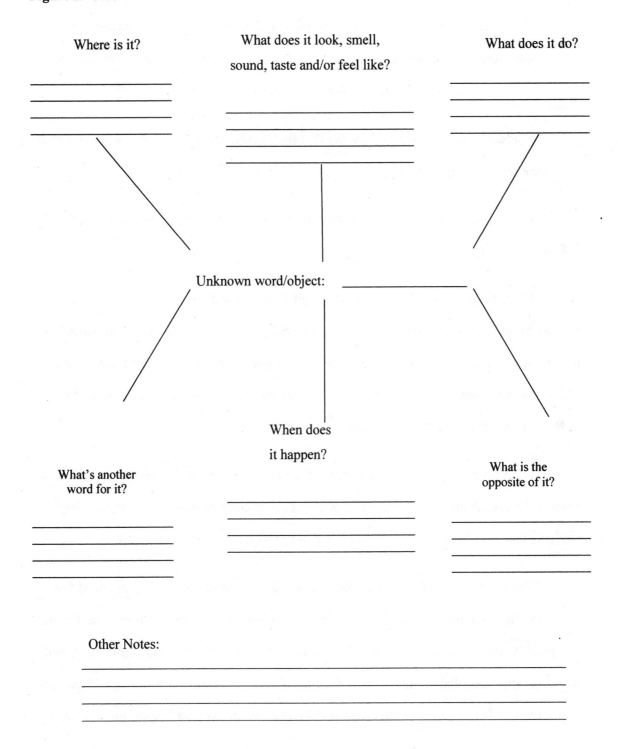

Where is it?

What does it look, smell, sound, taste and/or feel like?

What does it do?

Unknown word/object:

When does it happen?

What's another word for it?

What is the opposite of it?

Other Notes:

At this point, the teacher shows the video, gives students a few minutes to fill in clues on their Clue Webs, and then begins a dialogue with them.

"Was everyone able to get all of the information they needed to answer the questions after watching the video once? Did you catch all that the tour guide said?" "What would help you figure out even more of the answers?"

Students will almost certainly say that they could learn more if they could watch the tape again. If they don't, the teacher points this out and then replays the video.

After this, she asks for a volunteer to identify the place described in the video, which is Hawaii.

Next, the teacher asks students what clues suggested it was Hawaii. Likely responses include "Hawaiian music," "palm trees," "the beach," and "tropical fruits." The teacher writes these clues on the Clue Web and compliments students on their efforts. Then, she challenges them to identify more clues that this is Hawaii, and replays the video as many times as students request.

Each time the video is replayed, students record additional clues on their Clue Web and report them to the class. The goal is to demonstrate that the more carefully students watch and the more times they watch the more clues they can find.

The teacher concludes the introductory lesson by noting that finding all of the clues and figuring out that the place shown in the video was Hawaii required hard work and persistence, that each time they viewed the video again they found more clues, and that this same sort of sleuthing is what they need to do when they are trying to figure out unknown words they meet while reading. She goes on to say that beginning tomorrow they will learning a particular strategy—a powerful plan—for figuring out the meanings of unknown words they come across. And, she notes, they will find that the strategy is a lot like the approach they used to figure out that the place shown in the video was Hawaii.

Day 2—Introduction To Using Context Clues and the Four-Step Strategy

The teacher begins Day 2 with a brief review of what the class did on Day 1, and then moves quickly to the topic for the day, learning a powerful strategy for figuring out the meanings of unknown words they meet while reading.

"Today, we're going to learn a strategy for using clues to figure something out. But this strategy will not be for figuring out what place is shown in a video. Instead, it will be for figuring out the meanings of unknown words that we meet when we're reading."

"Actually, we won't exactly be 'figuring out' meanings. Instead, we'll be 'inferring meanings.' The strategy in called 'Inferring Word Meanings from Context.' When we infer something, we make an educated guess about it. And when we infer word meanings from context, we are making educated guesses about the meanings of the words. The context in which we find a word doesn't usually tell us the exact meaning of a word, but it often gives us a good idea of the word's meaning, and that is often enough to understand what we are reading."

At this point, the teacher puts up a large and colorful poster with the name of the strategy and the four steps, and begins discussing the strategy. A sample poster is shown in Figure 3.

Figure 3. Four-Step Strategy for Inferring Word Meanings from Context

▶ and **?**   1.   <u>Play and Question:</u>

Read carefully.
Frequently ask yourself, "Does this make sense?"

▮▶   2.   <u>Slow Advance:</u>

Notice when you don't know the meaning of a word and slow down.

Read that sentence at least once more, looking for clues.

■ and ◀◀   3.   <u>Stop and Rewind:</u>

If necessary, go back and reread, looking for clues that help you
figure out what the word might mean.

▶ and **?**   4.   <u>Play and Question:</u>

When you figure out what the word might mean, substitute your
guess in for the difficult word and see if it makes sense.

If it does, keep on reading.

If it doesn't, stop, rewind, and try again.

"Do you recognize this strategy?"

A number of students note that they do recognize it, that it is the VCR strategy
they worked with the day before.

"Right. This is the same strategy we used yesterday, but now we are applying it to figuring out unknown words we meet in reading rather than to figuring out an unknown place we see in a video. Here's how it works."

"As you can see, the first step in the strategy is Play and Question. That means you read carefully, always asking yourself if you are understanding what you are reading."

"Then, when you come to a word you don't know, you move to the second step—Slow Advance. At this point, you slow down, read the sentence at least once more looking for clues to the meaning of the word, and see if you can infer its meaning."

"If you can infer the word's meaning from just rereading the sentence, that's great. You continue to read. But if you can't infer the words meaning from reading the sentence, it's time to move to the third step of the strategy—Stop and Rewind. At this point you stop, go back, and read the sentence or two that comes before the one with the unknown word, again looking for clues to the meaning of the word."

"If you can now infer its meaning, excellent. You can move on to the fourth step of the strategy, which is also called Play and Question. But this time Play and Question means to try out the word you inferred. Substitute your educated guess for the word you didn't know and see if that works. If it does, keep on reading. If it doesn't, you'll need to Stop and Rewind again, ask someone about the word, look it up in the dictionary, or simply continue to read, understanding the passage as well as you can without knowing the meaning of the word."

"I know that all of this sounds pretty complicated. And using context clues to infer the meanings of unknown is going to take some work. But the work is well worth it because learning to use context clues helps to make you an independent and powerful reader, a reader who can read anything because you know what to do when unknown words come up. Don't worry if you don't understand the strategy well right now. We are going to spend two weeks on it, and together we can master it."

"Now it's time to try out the strategy. And remember that this is just the first of many times we'll do this, and I will be helping you all the way."

Sample Teacher-Student Dialogue. Shown below is a sample dialogue in which the teacher and the class work together to infer the meaning of a difficult word.

Teacher: "Much like we did with the video, we are going to take a small section of a book and make sure we understand it before moving on. I will read a paragraph aloud and then stop and check to make sure everyone understood the words and the ideas. The book is *The Phantom Tollbooth* by Norton Jester. As you will see, the story is set in a very strange place. Here is the paragraph we're going to work with.

> "A-H-H-H-R-R-E-M-M," roared the gateman, clearing his throat and snapping smartly to attention. "This is Dictionopolis, a happy kingdom, advantageously located in the Foothills of Confusion. The breezes come right off the Sea of Knowledge and cool the foothills gently. In this kingdom we don't have the cold temperatures like at the top of the mountains, nor the rain that the other side of the mountain gets.

Teacher: "This gateman is welcoming the main character, Milo, into his city of Dictionopolis. Notice that Foothills of Confusion and Sea of Knowledge are capitalized. What does that tell you?"

Students: "They're proper nouns." "They're names of places."

Teacher: "Exactly. Knowing what sorts of words are capitalized will help you understand this section."

Teacher: "Did everyone understand the paragraph completely? If we don't understand everything, what could we do?"

Students: "Reread it." "Read it again." "Read it slower." "Ask ourselves questions as we are reading it."

Teacher: "Good thinking. You used came up with two of the steps to our strategy, Slow Advance and Stop and Rewind. Let's use those two steps now. As I reread the sentence, listen for words that you don't know."

The teacher again reads the paragraph aloud.

Teacher: "Were there any difficult words in that sentence? If so, what were they?"

Students: "Advantageously."

Teacher: "Let's highlight that one. "Now, let's reread just the sentence that advantageously is in and the one after it. We don't need to reread the whole thing every time, just the section we're focusing on."

The teacher rereads just the one sentence.

Teacher: "Does advantageously sound like a positive thing?"

Students: "It does to me." "It says that it is a happy kingdom. I think that it has a positive meaning."

Teacher: "What are some of the things the paragraph tells us about this kingdom?"

Students: "That it gets nice breezes off the sea." "It's not as cold as the mountain peaks and it's not as rainy as the other side of the mountain."

Teacher: "Would that make it a pleasant place to live?"

Students. "Yes." "It's nice to have a breeze." "It's also good that it's not too cold." "And being not so rainy is a good thing too."

Teacher: "What is the word advantageously describing?"

Students: "Where this city is located."

Teacher: "That's right. The city is located in an advantageous place. What do you think that advantageous could mean?"

Students: "Nice?"

Teacher: "Let's add an -ly to that because our unknown word had an -ly. Then, let's write nicely above the word advantageously. Now, we should reread the paragraph with our replacement word to see if it makes sense. This time, while I'm reading, ask yourself if you understand what sort of place the story takes place in."

The teacher crosses out advantageously on the overhead and replaces it with nicely.

Teacher: "What do you think? Did nicely fit in the sentence OK? Does the sentence make sense now?"

Students: "Yes." "It does make sense." "Dictionopolis sounds like a good place to live."

Teacher: "I agree. I think that we now have a better understanding of the whole paragraph because we understand the word advantageously better. That's what learning to use context to infer word meanings can do. It can help us learn words, and it can help us better understand what we read."

Independent Practice. In addition to the Guided Practice illustrated in the teacher-student dialogue, each session from the second day of instruction on includes Independent Practice. This first Independent Practice is brief and does not require the students to do a lot on their own. The teacher gives them a brief paragraph with some difficult words, asks them to read it several times and mark any words they don't know or are uncertain of, and tells them they will discuss using the context clue strategy with this paragraph the next day. As the instruction continues, the Guided Practice portions of the lessons will become much shorter, and the Independent Practice sessions will become longer and more challenging.

Review and Question Session. Each session ends with a review and question session. The teacher reviews what students have learned that day and throughout the unit, primarily by calling on students to recap what they have learned. Each ending session also gives students an opportunity to ask questions and get clarification on anything they are uncertain of.

The Remaining Eight Days of Initial Instruction

As shown in Figure 1, over the next eight days, the class receives detailed instruction on the four-step strategy, interrupts the hard work with a game using the strategy, does guided practice with both narrative text and expository text, uses the strategy with authentic text, and makes plans for using the strategy in the future. There are also several important things that the figure cannot show: Increasingly, the students talk more and the teacher talks less. The students do more of the work. They take more responsibility for the strategy, and they increasingly self-monitor and self-regulate their use of the strategy. At the same time, the teacher is always there to support students' efforts, providing encouragement, scaffolding, and feedback as needed.

Transfer, Review, and Integration Activities

It is vital to realize that this initial unit of using context clues, substantial as it has been, is only the first step in assisting students in becoming competent and confident users of this important strategy. In the weeks, months, and years after the initial instruction, students need lots of independent practice, feedback, brief reviews and mini-lessons, opportunities to use the strategy, reminders to use it, and motivation to do so. It is only with such a long-term effort that students will fully learn the strategy, internalize it, and make it a part of their approach to building their vocabularies.

Teaching Students to Use Prefixes to Unlock the Meanings of Unknown Words

Taken with modifications from

"Teaching Prefixes: As Good as It Gets?"

by

Michael F. Graves

Published in J. F. Baumann & E. B. Kame'enui. *Vocabulary instruction: Research to practice* (pp. 81-99). New York: Guilford Press. Reprinted with permission.

While teaching students to use context clues is the most important word learning strategy to teach, teaching the to use word parts is a close second. In fact, about half the new words that students meet in their reading are related to familiar words. Once students can break words into parts, they can use their knowledge of word parts to attempt to deduce their meaning—if of course they understand word parts and how they function. Of the three types of word parts to consider teaching—prefixes, suffixes, and roots—prefixes are the most powerful elements to teach for the reasons shown below.

Why Prefixes are Particularly Worth Teaching

- There are relatively few prefixes to teach.

- They are used in a large number of words.

- They are consistently spelled.

- The appear at the beginnings of words, where they are easy for students to spot.

Here, we describe a procedure for teaching prefixes in detail.

Day 1—Introduction, Clarification, Motivation, and Overview

On Day 1, the teacher introduces the concept of prefixes and the strategy of using prefixes to unlock the meanings of unknown words, attempts to motivate students by stressing the value of prefixes, and gives students an overview of the unit. There has been a good deal of confusion about prefixes and prefix instruction, and thus it is particularly important to be sure that students understand just what prefixes and prefixed words are.

To alert students to what they will be studying and as a continuing reminder throughout the prefix unit, on the first day of instruction, the teacher puts up a poster advertising the instruction, perhaps something like:

Prefixes—One Key to Building Your Vocabularies

Then, the teacher might say something like this: "Over the next few days, we're going to be looking at how you can use prefixes to help you figure out the meanings of words you don't know. If you learn some common prefixes and how to use your knowledge of these prefixes to understand words that contain those prefixes, you're going to be able to figure out the meanings of a lot of new words. And, as you know, figuring out the meanings of words you don't know in a passage is an important step in understanding the passage."

Next, the teacher asks students what they already know about prefixes, reinforcing correct information students provide and gently suggesting that any incorrect information they give is not quite on target. The purpose here is to get students thinking about prefixes and to get them actively involved in the session. However, it is critical that student have a clear understanding of prefixes, and for this reason, the teacher follows the discussion with a presentation supported by an overhead transparency. Below is the transparency, which the teacher reads aloud to students.

Basic Facts about Prefixes

- A prefix is a group of letters that goes in front of a word. *Un-* is one prefix you have probably seen. It often means "not."

- Although you can list prefixes by themselves, as with *un-,* in stories or other things that we read, prefixes are attached to words. They don't appear by themselves. In *unhappy,* for example, the prefix *un-* is attached to the word *happy.*

- When a prefix is attached to a word, it changes the meaning of the word. For example, when the prefix *un-* is attached to the word *happy,* it makes the word *unhappy,* which means "not happy."

- It's important to remember that, for a group of letters to really be a prefix, when you remove them from the word, you still have a real word left. Removing the prefix *un-* from the word *unhappy* still leaves the word *happy*. That means it's a prefix. But if you remove the letters *un* from the word *uncle*, you are left with *cle*, which is not a word. This means that the *un* in *uncle* is not a prefix.

This is a lot for students to remember, too much in fact. For this reason, the teacher constructs a shortened version of these points on a "Basic Facts about Prefixes" poster, puts that up next to the poster advertising the unit, and tells students that the poster will stay up for them to refer to throughout the unit and even after that.

At this point, the teacher asks students if they know any additional prefixes, being generally accepting of their answers, but (assuming that some responses are incorrect) noting afterwards that some of the elements given are not actually prefixes and that the class will continue to work on what is and what is not a prefix as the unit progresses.

Finally, the teacher introduces the three prefixes for study the next day—*un-* (not), *re-* (again), and *in-* (not)—putting them on an overhead, asking students to copy them down, and asking students to each bring in a word beginning with one of the prefixes the next day.

Day 2—Instruction on the First Three Prefixes

At the beginning of the session, the teacher refers to the "Basic Facts" posters, briefly reminding students what prefixes are, where they appear, and why it is important to know about them. Then, the teacher calls on some students to give the prefixed words they have located, jotting those that are indeed prefixed words on the board, and gently noting that the others are not actually prefixed words and that they will discuss them later.

After this, the teacher begins the standard instructional routine for teaching prefixes and prefix removal. We suggest this standardized routine for three reasons First, there is experimental evidence that it works. Second, using the same routine for teaching all six prefixes means that students can soon learn the procedure itself and then concentrate on the learning the prefixes and how to work with them. Third, the routine suggested can serve as a model teachers can use in creating a complete set of materials for teaching prefixes and the strategy of prefix removal and replacement.

Next, the teacher tells students that today they will be working with the three prefixes introduced the day before and how to use them in unlocking the meanings of unknown words. The three prefixes are *un-* meaning "not," *re-* meaning "again," and *in-* also meaning "not." In teaching these three prefixes, the teacher will use several types of materials—transparencies introducing each prefix, worksheets with brief exercises requiring use of the prefix just taught, transparencies of these worksheets, exercise sheets requiring additional use and manipulation of each prefix, and review sheets on which students manipulate the three prefixes and the words that were used in illustrating the prefixes for the day. On the back of the worksheets, exercise sheets, and review sheets are answer keys so that student can immediately check their efforts.

Each introductory transparency presents one prefix, illustrates its use with two familiar words and two unfamiliar words, and uses each of the four words in a context-rich sentence. Below each sentence, the word and its definition are shown. And below these sample sentences, is a fifth sentence, which gives students a root word and requires them to generate the prefixed form of the word. The introductory transparency for the prefix *re-* is shown in Figure 1.

Figure 1. Introductory Transparency for the Prefix re-

THE PREFIX <u>RE-</u>

1. Tom was asked to <u>rewrite</u> his spelling test a second time.

rewrite — to write again

2. Carmen had to <u>repeat</u> her joke because her grandfather did not hear it

repeat — to say again

3. After the heavy doors were battered by the enemy, the soldiers rushed to <u>refortify</u> their stronghold.

refortify — to make strong again

4. The original movie had bee a big hit, so they decided to <u>remake</u> it with some current stars.

remake — to make again

5. If <u>commence</u> means "begin," then <u>recommence</u> means

---

Instruction begins with the teacher displaying the first sentence on the introductory transparency and leading students from the meaning of the familiar prefixed word to the meaning of the prefix itself as illustrated on the next page:

Teacher: If Tom were asked to rewrite a test, what must he do?

Students: He has to take it over. He has to take it again.

Teacher: That's correct. Using your understanding of the word *rewrite*,
             what is the meaning of the prefix *re-*?

Students: Again. A second time. Over again.

The process is repeated with the next three sentences on the transparency. With some prefixes, students are likely to be able to volunteer the response without difficulty. With others, they may need further prompting, in which case the teacher rephrases the sentence to add more clues. If students are still unable to respond after the prompting, the teacher gives the definition. After going through the first four sentences on the *re-* introductory overhead, the teacher presents the fifth sentence, which defines the unknown root word and asks students to define the prefixed word.

After completing introductory instruction on the first prefix, students individually complete their check sheets, while a student volunteer completes the check sheet on a transparency. Part of a check sheet is shown in Figure 2. As soon as students complete their check sheets, the volunteer puts the transparency on the overhead so that all students receive immediate feedback on their work. If the volunteer has made an error, the teacher corrects it at this time.

Figure 2. Part of a Check Sheet for the Prefix sub-

CAN YOU FIND IT?

A word or prefix is hidden in each line of letters below. Read the definition of the word or prefix. Then circle the word or prefix when you find it.

1. Find the prefix meaning "under" or "below"

   antidissubplegohnobitto

2. Find the word in each line that means:

   a. "underground railroad"

      shelaunomessubwaywathoning

   b. "to put under water"

      lasubmergersinthergerows

   c. "a plot beneath the main plot"

      thisenroutelesubplotrudiw

   d. "underwater boat"

      mopeitaqksubmarinetshowl

These same procedures are then completed with the two remaining prefixes for the day—*un-* and *in-*. Following initial instruction on the three prefixes, the students complete a review sheet and immediately receive feedback by checking the answers on the back of the sheet. Part of a review sheet is shown in Figure 3. While students are completing the review sheet, the teacher monitors their work and provides assistance when requested. This concludes the second day of the unit.

Figure 3. Part of a Review Sheet for the Prefixes un-, re-, and in-

REVIEW SHEET ON UN-, RE-, AND IN-

A. Match the prefix in the first column to its meaning in the second column.

    a.   re-   _____ not

    b.   in-   _____ again

    c.   un-   _____ not

B. Complete the following sentences with a word from the list below. You will not use every word.

    rewrite   inaudible   incomplete

    reconnect   unhappy   ungrateful

1. Because Feng-Yi was in such a hurry to finish her test before the bell rang, her last answer was _____ .

2. A nearly _____ cry escaped her as she hid behind the curtain.

Day 3—Review, the Prefix Strategy, and the Remaining Three Prefixes

Day 3 begins with the teacher reviewing the basic facts about prefixes on the poster. Then students complete a review sheet on the three prefixes taught the previous day and immediately correct their work.

Next comes another crucial part of the instruction—instruction in the prefix strategy. The teacher introduces the strategy by telling students that now that they have worked some with the strategy and understand how useful prefixes can be in figuring out the meanings of unknown words, the teacher is going to teach a specific strategy for

working with unknown words. The teacher titles the procedure "Prefix Removal and Replacement," emphasizing that they are using a big name for an important idea.

The teacher then puts up the "Prefix Removal and Replacement" transparency, which is reproduced on a prominently displayed "Prefix Removal and Replacement Strategy" poster, and talks students through the procedure with one or two sample prefixed words.

The Prefix Removal and Replacement Strategy

When you come to an unknown word that may contain a prefix:

- Remove the "prefix."

- Check that you have a real word remaining. If you do, you've found a prefix.

- Think about the meaning of the prefix and the meaning of the root word.

- Combine the meanings of the prefix and the root word, and infer the meaning of the unknown word.

- Try out the meaning of the "unknown" word in the sentence, and see if it makes sense. If it does, read on. If it doesn't, you'll need to use another strategy for discovering the unknown word's meaning.

Following this explicit description of the strategy and modeling of its use, the teacher tells students that they will continue to work on learning the meanings of prefixes and learning to use the strategy today, tomorrow, and in future review sessions. The teacher then points out to students that they now have two posters to refer to when they come to an unknown word that may contain a prefix—the "Basic Facts" poster and the "Prefix Strategy" poster. Finally, the teacher teaches and reviews the remaining three prefixes—*dis-, en-,* and *non*—using procedures and materials that exactly parallel those used on Day 2. This concludes the third day of the unit.

Day 4—Review of the Information about Prefixes, the Prefix Strategy, and the Prefixes Taught

Day 4 begins with the teacher reviewing the four facts about prefixes, again using the "Basic Facts" poster in doing so. As part of the review, the teacher asks students a few questions about these facts to be sure they understand them and answers any questions students have.

Next, the teacher reviews the prefix removal and replacement strategy using the "Prefix Strategy" poster. After this, the teacher continues with the explicit instruction model, first modeling use of the strategy with two of the six prefixes taught and then collaboratively using the strategy in a whole-class session with two more of the six prefixes. After this, the teacher divides students into small groups and provides guided practice by having the groups use the strategy with the final pair of prefixes. The teacher also has some of the groups share their work and their findings, thus providing guided practice.

As the final activity of the initial instruction, small groups of students work together on a quiz. The quiz requires them to state the four facts about prefixes, state the steps of the prefix removal and replacement strategy, and give the meanings of the six prefixes taught. As soon as students complete the quiz, they correct the quiz in class so that they get immediate feedback on their performance and hand the corrected quizzes in so that the teacher has this information to plan reviews.

Reviewing, Prompting, and Guiding Students to Independence

At this point, the instruction is far from complete. If we really want students to remember what a prefix is, recognize and know the meanings of some prefixes, and use the prefix removal and replacement strategy when they come to unknown words in their reading, reviewing what has been taught, prompting student to use the strategy in materials they are reading, and generally continuing to nudge then toward independence are crucial.

By reviewing, we mean formal reviews. It would seem reasonable to have the first review about a month after the initial instruction, a second review something like two months after that, and a third review, if it seems necessary, several months after that. Each review might last 30-45 minutes. Two somewhat conflicting considerations are important in undertaking these reviews. The first is that it does no good and in all probability does some harm to spend time "teaching" students things they already know. Thus, if at the beginning of a review, it is apparent that students already know the material, the review should be very brief. The second consideration is that we need to do our best to ensure that all students understand prefixes and the prefix removal and replacement strategy. It is not enough if only average and better readers get it.

By prompting, we simply mean reminding students about prefixes and the prefix strategy at appropriate points. Thus, when students are about to read a selection that contains some unknown prefixed words, the teacher might say something like, "In looking through today's reading, I noticed some pretty hard words that begin with prefixes. Be on the lookout for these, and if you don't know them, try using the prefix strategy to figure out their meanings." This sort of prompting should probably be fairly frequent, for it can do a lot to move students toward independent use of the strategy.

Instruction in Additional Prefixes and Additional Review and Prompting

As noted earlier, it seems reasonable to teach the 20 most frequent prefixes over a three-year period. Thus, following the frequency list presented in *Teaching Reading in the 21st Century,* the prefixes *in-* ("in" or "into") through *fore-* might be taught in fifth grade, and the prefixes *de-* through *under-* might be taught in sixth grade. Such instruction would be similar to that used with the initial six prefixes, with one very important exception. Students will have already been taught the basic facts about prefixes and the prefix removal and replacement strategy; work on those matters is review and can be briefer than the initial instruction.

Finally, reviewing and prompting is still important during fifth and sixth grades. Again, two reviews—cumulative reviews of all the prefixes taught as well as the basic facts about prefixes and the prefix strategy—seem likely to be sufficient. And again, it is important to keep in mind that the goal is to ensure that all students know the prefixes and can use the strategy without boring students by teaching them what they already know.

Scaffolded Reading Experience[TM] for Fostering Higher Order Reading and Comprehension Skills

with

Because of Winn-Dixie

by Kate DiCamillo

Created by Lauren A. Liang
University of Minnesota,
© 2003 Seward Learning Systems, Inc.
Available at OnLine Reading Resources
onlinereadingresources.com

Table of Contents

Introduction

> "Take one disarmingly engaging protagonist and put her in the company
> of a tenderly rendered canine, and you've got yourself a recipe for the best
> kind of down-home literary treat. Kate DiCamillo's voice in *Because of
> Winn-Dixie* should carry from the steamy, sultry pockets of Florida clear
> across the miles to enchant young readers everywhere."
> > *-Karen Hesse*

With the support of the 1998 McKnight Artist Fellowship for Writers and a local writing group, author Kate DiCamillo wove an engaging story for children starring thoughtful, 10-year old India Opal and her beloved friend and pet dog, Winn-Dixie. The resulting book, *Because of Winn-Dixie*, has received much praise, including being named as a 2001 Newbery Honor book and a 2001 Riverbank Review Children's Book of Distinction.

The well-developed characters, universal themes of friendships and grief, and the lyrical prose of the novel have helped make it very popular with children in the intermediate grades. The protagonist, Opal, is a lonely child and searches for friends in the new town to which she and her father have recently moved. The diversity of the friends she gradually makes—from an elderly librarian to a guitar-playing ex-felon who works in the local pet store—and the way she brings them together as a community make for an entertaining tale.

This Scaffolded Reading Experience focuses on these strengths of the novel, making use of DiCamillo's rich and memorable cast of characters. The SRE is designed to help students develop the skills of identifying character traits and distinguish between personal attributes and physical traits, and to see clearly how authors develop the personality of their characters. Students are asked to use textual quotes as "evidence" of certain traits of individual characters. The SRE was developed particularly for fifth and sixth graders, and uses strategies such as partner and group work, repeated trials at various tasks, and practice at reading skills such as making predictions.

Objectives

- To introduce students to two types of character traits: personal attributes and physical traits

- To give students experience using textual quotes to support an opinion or judgment

- To give students experience making predictions in fiction stories

- To help develop students' awareness of character development in novels

Higher-Order Thinking Skills

- Understanding — Constructing meaning from instructional messages, including oral, written, and graphic communications.

- Analyzing — Breaking material into its constituent parts and determining how the parts relate to one another and to an overall structure or purpose.

- Evaluating — Making judgments based on criteria and standards.

Chronological List of Activities

Day 1

Prereading Activity

1. Relating the Reading to Students' Lives *20 minutes*

During Reading Activity

1. Reading to Students *20- 25 minutes*

During Reading Activity (as homework)

1. Silent Reading *as homework*

Day 2

Postreading Activity

1. Questioning *5 minutes*

Prereading Activities

1. Preteaching Concepts *20 minutes*

2. Direction Setting *15 minutes*

During Reading Activity (as homework)

1. Silent Reading *as homework*

Postreading Activity (as homework)

1. Writing *as homework*

Day 3

Postreading Activity

1. Discussion *10 minutes*

Prereading Activity

1. Predicting *10 minutes*

During Reading Activity

1. Reading to Students *15 minutes*

Prereading Activity

1. Predicting *5 minutes*

During Reading Activity (as homework)

1. Silent Reading *as homework*

Postreading Activity (as homework)

1. Writing *as homework*

Day 4

Postreading Activity

1. Graphic Activity *45 minutes*

Prereading Activity

1. Building Background Knowledge *5 minutes*

During Reading Activity (as homework)

1. Silent Reading *as homework*

Postreading Activity (as homework)

1. Writing *as homework*

Day 5

Postreading Activity

1. Discussion *5 minutes*

During Reading Activity

1. Reading to Students *15 minutes*

Post Reading Activity

1. Discussion *20 minutes*

During Reading Activity (as homework)

1. Silent Reading *as homework*

Postreading Activity (as homework)

1. Writing *as homework*

Day 6

Postreading Activities

1. Drama and Writing *40 minutes*

2. Discussion *5 minutes*

Prereading Activity

1. Predicting *5 minutes*

During Reading Activity (as homework)

1. Silent Reading *as homework*

Postreading Activity (as homework)

1. Writing *as homework*

Day 7

Postreading Activity

1. Discussion *10 minutes*

Prereading Activity

1. Predicting *5 minutes*

During Reading Activity

1. Reading to Students *25 minutes*

During Reading Activity (as homework)

1. Silent Reading *as homework*

Postreading Activity (as homework)

1. Writing *as homework*

Day 8

Postreading Activity

1. Discussion *10 minutes*

During Reading Activity

1. Reading to Students *15 minutes*

Postreading Activities

1. Questioning *20 minutes*

Day 9-10 and as homework

Postreading Activities

1. Artistic and Graphic Activities and Writing *60-120 minutes*

2. Discussion *20- 30 minutes*

Optional Additional Activities

Postreading Activity

1. Artistic and Graphic Activities, Writing, and/or Drama

Detailed Description of Activities

Day 1

Prereading Activity

1. Relating the Reading to Student's Lives 20 minutes

Hand out the story preview to students and read it aloud together. (See Student Materials.) Then have students write for five minutes about a time they experienced moving or being the newcomer in a situation at camp, school, etc. After five minutes of writing, have students share their writing with a partner in a two minute pair-share (In a two-minute pair-share, each student has two minutes to talk without any interruptions about what they wrote. After each partner has had two minutes, allow two minutes for students to ask one another questions or offer comments.) Then ask students to share to the whole group if they so desire.

Next, brainstorm as a whole class ways to make new friends when you are new to a place. After generating a short list of possibilities, tell students the book they are about to read is about a 10 year old girl who moves to a new town in Florida, and the experiences she has as she gets used to her new surroundings and makes friends, as well as dealing with some of the past experiences she has had in her life.

During Reading Activity

1. Reading to Students 20-25 minutes

Have students open their books and follow along as you read aloud the first two chapters. Discuss the definition of "missionary" when you come across the word. You may also need to describe "Winn-Dixie" if students are unfamiliar with the store.

During Reading Activity (as homework)

1.   *Silent Reading*

Have students read Chapters 3 and 4 for homework.

Day 2

Postreading Activity

1. *Questioning 5 minutes*

On the board or overhead, have students help write the list of 10 things Opal finds out about her mother.

Prereading Activities

1. *Preteaching Concepts 20 minutes*

Ask students which of the items are physical traits; that is, things that describe Mama's physical appearance. Label these items "P. T." Then have students look at the remaining items. Explain that these items describe Mama in a different way: They are all examples of personal attributes Mama has. Tell students that when we describe a person, we often use both physical traits and personal attributes. For example, Brian is tall with brown hair and very patient with younger children. Then ask students, "How does an author let the reader get to know a character?" Brainstorm ideas, ultimately leading students to see that authors, most of the time, develop characters through physical descriptions, dialogue with others, inner thoughts, and actions. Through these ways, we get a picture of that character and his or her personality. Tell students that while they read this book, they are going to be looking and talking about the "character traits" of the characters. They'll be finding quotes in the story that show physical traits and personal attributes each character has.

Have students practice this idea of using physical traits and personal attributes for description by choosing a person they know well (their mom or dad, brother or sister, or best friend) and making a list of 5 physical traits and 5 personal attributes of that person. Circle the room and check students' work to see if they have the right idea. Have students share some of the personal attributes they came up with. Then pass out the list of possible Personal Attributes (See Student Materials.) Explain that this is only a partial list and that they should add more ideas to the list.

Now ask student to think about the character of Opal. Based on what they have read so far, what personal attributes does Opal have? As students suggest ideas, ask them to explain why they think that attribute fits and back up their reason with a specific quote from the book. You will likely need to guide students to find quotes. For example, if a student suggests Opal is brave because she saved Winn-Dixie from the pound, have students look at page 9 and 10 and find the quote that supports this idea: "Wait a minute!" I hollered. "That's my dog. Don't call the pound." All the Winn-Dixie employees turned around and looked at me, and I knew I had done something big. And maybe stupid, too. But I couldn't help it. I couldn't let that dog go to the pound."

2. *Direction Setting 15 minutes*

Pass out the Double-Entry Journal guide (See Student Materials) to students. Read through the guide with students and explain they will be responsible for doing an entry for each chapter assigned for homework. They must do personal attributes and not physical traits, and should do two for each chapter (These do not have to be for the same character.) Demonstrate an example on the board or overhead using a personal attribute for Opal that was just suggested.

During Reading Activity (as homework)

1.   Silent Reading

Have students read Chapters 5 and 6 for homework.

Postreading Activity

1.   Writing

Students should write in their double entry journals for each chapter (Two personal attributes with textual evidence per chapter.)

Day 3

Postreading Activity

1. Discussion 10 minutes

Begin by having students briefly share their double-entry journal assignments, either with partners or in small groups. Ask a few students to volunteer examples to the whole class.

Then as a whole class, briefly discuss Opal's adaptation to her new town so far. Does it seem like she has made any new friends?

Prereading Activity

1. Predicting 10 minutes

Give students three or four minutes to write down their predictions of what Miss Fanny's story might be. Share a few of these ideas as a whole class

During Reading Activity

1. Reading to Students 15 minutes

Read aloud Chapter 7 to the students while they follow along.

Prereading Activity

1. Predicting 5 minutes

Have students make predictions about Amanda and the role she will play in the book.

During Reading Activity (as homework)

1.   Silent Reading

Have students read Chapters 8, 9, and 10 for homework.

Postreading Activity (as homework)

1.   Writing

Students should write in their double-entry journals for each chapter. (Two personal attributes with textual evidence for each chapter.)

Day 4

Postreading Activity

1. Graphic Activity 45 minutes

Have students in partner groups create a list of all the characters in the book so far. For each character, they should list two personal attributes next to the character's name. Next to these two traits, have the students draw the character, showing two physical traits in the picture.

Have students share their work with each other.

Prereading Activity

1.   *Building Background Knowledge 5 minutes*

        Discuss briefly with students how animals often react to storms.

During Reading Activity (as homework)

   1.   *Silent Reading*

        Have students read Chapters 11, 12, and 13 for homework.

Postreading Activity (as homework)

   1.   *Writing*

             Students should write in their double-entry journals for each chapter. (Two personal attributes with textual evidence for each chapter.)

Day 5

Postreading Activity

   1.   *Discussion 5 minutes*

        Ask students to share one of the personal attributes they discovered in last night's reading, and the textual evidence they wrote down as the supportive quote.

During Reading Activity

   1.   *Reading to Students 15 minutes*

        Read aloud Chapter 14 to students as they follow along.

Postreading Activity

   1.   *Discussion 20 minutes*

        Have students reread the lines on page 96 that say "Judge them by what they are doing now." Then ask students if they would rather be judged by what they are doing right now or by what they were like in the past. Have students debate this idea in small groups and then as a whole class.

During Reading Activity (as homework)

1. Silent Reading

Have students read Chapters 15, 16, and 17 for homework.

Postreading Activity (as homework)

1. Writing

Students should write in their double-entry journals for each chapter. (Two personal attributes with textual evidence for each chapter.)

Day 6

Postreading Activities

1. Writing and Drama 40 minutes

On the board or overhead, write the word "bittersweet." Give students 10 to 15 minutes to write about an experience in their lives that they would call "bittersweet." After the writing time is over, have students share their stories with small groups. Then have each small group of students choose one story to act out in a brief skit for the class. Allow a few of the groups to act out their stories for the class.

2. Discussion 5 minutes

As a whole class, briefly discuss why India Opal's life is "bittersweet."

Prereading Activity

1. Predicting 5 minutes

Have students predict what they think will happen next in the story.

During Reading Activity (as homework)

1. *Silent Reading*

Have students read Chapters 18, 19, and 20 for homework.

Postreading Activity (as homework)

1. Writing

Students should write in their double-entry journals for each chapter. (Two personal attributes with textual evidence for each chapter.)

Day 7

Postreading Activity

1. Discussion 10 minutes

Have students pull out their double-entry journal assignments. Looking at what they have written, does it look like any of the characters have changed and may show different personal attributes than they did before? Have students give examples from the text that show characters may have changed.

Prereading Activity

1. Predicting 5 minutes

Have students predict what will happen at the party.

During Reading Activity

1. Reading to Students 25 minutes

Read aloud chapters 21 and 22 to your students.

During Reading Activity (as homework)

1. *Silent Reading*

Have students read Chapters 23, 24, and 25 for homework.

Postreading Activity (as homework)

1. Writing

Students should write in their double-entry journals for each chapter. (Two personal attributes with textual evidence for each chapter.)

Day 8

Postreading Activity

1. Discussion 10 minutes

Have students share with partners their favorite parts of the last four chapters in the book. Share a few of these as a whole class.

During Reading Activity

1. Reading to Students 15 minutes

Read aloud Chapter 26 to students.

Postreading Activity

1. Questioning 20 minutes

Have students respond in writing to two questions:
    (1) Why is 10 things not enough?
    (2) Do you think the ending is positive or negative? Why?
If time allows, you may want to discuss these questions orally.

Days 9-10

Postreading Activities

1. *Graphic and Artistic Activities and Writing 60 –120 minutes and as homework*

   As a final activity for the book, have students work on the following assignment in class and as homework: "Make a poster featuring one of the characters in the story. The poster must contain a picture of the character exhibiting three physical traits that were mentioned in the story. These traits should be labeled and a quote from the text written by the label as "evidence." Underneath the picture, list five personal attributes of the character with a quote from the text to support each attribute. At the very bottom of the poster, write what is "bittersweet" for that character." (See Student Materials.)

2. *Discussion 20-30 minutes*

   Allow students to view one another's posters and make positive comments. One way you can do this is to have students place their posters on their desks and rotate seats every few minutes. A piece of paper left at the desk can be used for the "visiting" students to write a positive comment.

Optional Additional Activities

1. Write an essay about an experience you have had that is bittersweet. [Note: This essay can be used as part of the Personal Narrative Minnesota Graduation Standard for the Intermediate Level (Write and Speak.)]

2. Read Kate DiCamillo's newest book, *The Tiger Rising* (Candlewick Press, 2001.) How is it bittersweet? Compare India Opal to Rob of *The Tiger Rising.*

3. Draw a picture of one of the scenes in the book that you think is very important to revealing one of the character's personality traits. Explain in writing why you think this scene is important for that reason.

4. Write a song (lyrics only to a tune you know or the tune and the lyrics) that Oliver might sing to his pets in the store. Explain why you think Oliver would sing this song.

Student Materials

Student materials for *Because of Winn-Dixie* include a preview, a possible personal attributes (character traits)" handout, a *Because of Winn-Dixie* double-entry journal handout, and a *Because of Winn-Dixie* final project.

- Preview for *Because of Winn-Dixie*. A preview (Graves, Prenn, & Cooke, 1985) is a well-crafted introduction to a text that is read to students prior to their reading the text itself. Previews include an introduction designed to gain students' attention, an overview of the text up to a suitable stopping place, and brief directions for reading.

- *Because of Winn-Dixie* Possible Personal Attributes (Character Traits) Handout. This handout lists attributes that characters might have.

- *Because of Winn-Dixie* Double-Entry Journal Handout. A form for listing character traits and quotes indicating those traits.

- *Because of Winn-Dixie* Final Project. Instructions for creating the final project, a poster with specific characteristics.

Preview for *Because of Winn-Dixie*

Have you ever moved to a new town? Or transferred to a new school with very few people you know? Or maybe gone to a summer camp away from home? Most people at one point or another have experienced what it is like to be new to a place. Perhaps the biggest challenge of being the newcomer is making friends. Think back to a time when you were the new person. How did it feel to not know anyone? Did you try to start conversations with others? Did you watch people closely? Can you remember what it felt like when you first met someone who might be a friend?

In *Because of Winn-Dixie*, you will meet India Opal, a ten-year-old girl who has just moved to a new town in Florida. You'll go along with her as she begins to get used to her new home and make friends. You will hear her first impressions of the people she meets, and see if any of those impressions change. You may also see that moving to the new town could change Opal, too.

Because of Winn-Dixie Possible Personal Attributes (Character Traits) Handout

Agreeable	Enthusiastic	Kind	Self-sacrificing
Aggressive	Fearless	Lazy	Self-centered
Ambitious	Flexible	Loyal	Selfish
Angry	Foolish	Merciful	Sensible
Appreciative	Friendly	Mischievous	Serious
Arrogant	Generous	Modest	Servile
Bashful	Gentle	Narrow-minded	Shy
Boastful	Grouchy	Noble	Stubborn
Brave	Gullible	Obedient	Subservient
Calculating	Hard-working	Observant	Superstitious
Candid	Honest	Overconfident	Suspicious
Cautious	Honorable	Patient	Thoughtful
Clever	Humble	Perceptive	Thoughtless
Conceited	Humorous	Persistent	Timid
Confident	Imaginative	Proud	Trusting
Considerate	Impatient	Reasonable	Uncooperative
Cooperative	Impulsive	Reliable	Understanding
Courageous	Inconsiderate	Responsible	Unreasonable
Curious	Independent	Rigid	Unselfish
Deceitful	Industrious	Sarcastic	Wise
Determined	Insecure	Scornful	
Dishonest	Insincere	Self-conscious	

***Because of Winn-Dixie* Double-Entry Journal Assignment**

For each chapter of Kate DiCamillo's *Because of Winn-Dixie* you will create
a page in your character double-entry journal. Use the format below and the sample
entry to help you.

Today's Date:

Chapter:

Character's Name and Personal Attribute	Quote from Text Showing This Personal Attribute
Name of character: Personal Attribute:	Page Number of Quote: Quote: " " Why this Quote Works:
Character's Name and Personal Attribute	Quote from Text Showing This Personal Attribute
Name of character: Personal Attribute:	Page Number of Quote: Quote: " " Why this Quote Works:

Sample Entry for Double-Entry Journal

Today's Date: *April 13*

Chapter: *15*

Character's Name and Personal Attribute	Quote from Text Showing This Personal Attribute
Name of character: *Opal* Personal Attribute: *considerate*	Page Number of Quote: *p. 100* Quote: *"I worried about him hogging the fan."* Why this Quote Works: *This quote shows that Opal is worried that her dog, Winn-Dixie, is sitting in front of the fan and Miss Fanny might not get any of the cool air from the fan. Since it is Miss Fanny's library and her fan, Opal doesn't want her dog, who is a guest, to hog all the fan.*

Because of Winn-Dixie **Final Project**

As a culminating activity after reading Kate DiCamillo's *Because of Winn-Dixie*, you are to create a special poster for one character of your choice. The poster must contain a picture of the character exhibiting three physical traits that were mentioned in the story. These traits should be labeled and a quote from the text written by the label as "evidence." Underneath the picture, list five personal attributes of the character with a quote from the text to support each attribute. At the very bottom of the poster, write what is "bittersweet" for that character."

Checklist for Final Project

Name of Character:

Put a check mark by each step when you complete it.

1. Picture of character.

2. Three physical traits of character labeled on picture.

3. Quote from text for each physical trait next to label.

4. List of five personal attributes of character.

5. Quote from text for each personal attribute labeled.

6. Paragraph written on bottom of poster explaining what is "bittersweet" for the character.

Sources of the Reading Selection, Additional Readings, and Other Material

Sources of the Reading Selection

DiCamillo, Kate. *Because of Winn-Dixie*. New York: Candlewick Press, 2000. 182 pp.

DiCamillo, Kate. *The Tiger Rising*. New York: Candlewick Press, 2001. 116 pp.

Criticism/Book Reviews

Engberg, Gillian. *Because of Winn-Dixie*. Booklist. May 1, 2000, Volume 96, Number 17, p. 1665.

James, Helen Foster. *Because of Winn-Dixie*. School Library Journal. June 2000, Volume 46, Number 6, p. 143.

Because of Winn-Dixie. The Horn Book Magazine. July 2000, Volume 76, Number 4, p. 455.

Internet Sites

http://childrensbooks.about.com/parenting/childrensbooks/library/weekly/aa040801a.htm — Summary of chat with Kate DiCamillo.

www.bookjackets.com — A short bit of information about Kate DiCamillo on the favorite authors page.

Reference

Graves, M. F., Prenn, M. C., & Cooke, C. L. (1985). The coming attraction: Previewing short stories to increase comprehension. Journal of Reading, 28, 594-598.

The First Two Days of Instruction on the Comprehension Strategy of Using Prior Knowledge

by

Michael F. Graves

Teaching comprehension strategies—teaching strategies such as establishing a purpose for reading, using prior knowledge, asking and answering questions, making inferences, determining what is important, summarizing, dealing with graphic information, imaging and creating graphic representations, and monitoring comprehension—is important at all grade levels. While instruction in kindergarten and the primary grades is certainly not as sophisticated as that in the higher grades, it is nevertheless vital to emphasize the importance of comprehension even in the earliest grades. Described below are the first two days of a unit on building prior knowledge as it might be presented to kindergarten students.

The First Day's Instruction on Using Prior Knowledge

The activities described here are those used on the first day of instruction on a new strategy. In this illustration, the students are kindergartners and the strategy to be taught is using prior knowledge. This is the first time it is formally taught. The first day's instruction includes four different components.

Motivation and Interest Building (about 5 minutes). To capture students' attention and build interest, introduce the strategy by having students tell you what they know about caterpillars.

Teacher Explanation (about 5 minutes). After students have shared several examples, explain that identifying what you already know about something is part of a strategy you are going to teach them. Explain that the strategy they will learn—using prior knowledge—will help them to better understand and remember what they read.

Teacher Modeling (about 5 minutes). Reveal more about how the strategy works by reading the first page of Eric Carle's *The Very Hungry Caterpillar*, "In the light of the moon a little egg lay on a leaf." Model the thought processes you might go through in using prior knowledge.

Let's see, what do I know about caterpillars? They like leaves. I've seen lots of tiny white dots on leaves before I see caterpillars. Maybe those dots are eggs. Some animals come from an egg. Maybe this egg will turn into a caterpillar.

Once you have explained the strategy and modeled it, check to see if students were following you by asking a few students to explain the strategy and tell why it is worth knowing.

Large Group Student Participation and Teacher Mediation (about 10 minutes). Read aloud several pages from a picture book that deals with a topic students will have some knowledge about. The sample paragraph below is taken from *The Very Hungry Caterpillar*, one book that meets this criterion.

Now he wasn't hungry any more—and he wasn't a little caterpillar any more. He was a big, fat caterpillar. He built a small house, called a cocoon, around himself. He stayed inside for more than two weeks. Then he nibbled a hole in the cocoon, pushed his way out and . . . ."

Ask students what they know about caterpillars (they eat leaves, they build a cocoon). Next, ask them what the story told them that went beyond what they already knew (caterpillars eat a lot, they live in the cocoon for two weeks, caterpillars nibble their way out of the cocoon). Have students continue to connect new details from the story with what they already knew.

Explain to students that they can often use something that they already know to help them understand something new. For example, they already knew caterpillars build a cocoon, but now they also know that they stay in it for two weeks and nibble their way out.

Thus far, this introductory session has lasted about 25 minutes. If that is too long for your kindergarteners, you might leave the Large Group Student Participation and

Teacher Mediation for the second day. But if you can get all of this in on one day, that is probably worth doing because these four activities make a nice introductory package.

The Second Day's Instruction on Using Prior Knowledge

Very briefly review the first day's lesson, again discussing what the strategy of using prior knowledge is, motivating students by reminding them how helpful the strategy will be for understanding and remembering what they read, and modeling your thought processes as you use prior knowledge when reading another book.

More Large Group Student Participation and Teacher Mediation (10 - 15 minutes). Work together with students to list some of the information they knew and learned about caterpillars yesterday (they come from an egg, they eat a lot of leaves, they build a cocoon and stay in it for two weeks, they nibble their way out of the cocoon and turn into a butterfly).

Now, read the first four pages of Linda Glaser's *Magnificent Monarchs,* another book that involves caterpillars.

> Look what I found here in these weeds. A shiny white egg stuck on a leaf. A tiny monarch caterpillar pushes her way our, my soft wiggly friend. She eats and eats the milkweed leaves. She grows and grows until she grows right out of her small tight skin. She now has a bigger looser one. She eats more and more milkweed and then ...she grows right out of her skin again ...and again ... and again.

Ask students to use their prior knowledge to point out some of the things they already knew about caterpillars (comes from an egg, eats a lot of leaves). Then ask students to tell you what new information they learned (the egg sticks to the leaf, the caterpillar pushes out of the egg, the caterpillar gets new skin as it grows).

As students begin to understand the idea of using what they already know to understand the new information, they should do more and more of the identifying of the information themselves and receive less and less modeling by you.

This would conclude the first two day's of instruction and practice with the strategy. The remainder of the unit is discussed after the first two days of instruction of a unit on Determining What is Important are described in *Teaching Reading in the 21st Century* 4/E.

A Description of Questioning the Author (QtA), an Approach to Teaching for Understanding Developed by Isable Beck and Margaret McKeown

by

Michael F. Graves

Questioning the Author is a large-group questioning and discussion procedure developed and validated by Isabel Beck and Margaret McKeown (Beck, McKeown, Hamilton, & Kucan, 1997, 1998; Beck, McKeown, Worthy, Sandora, & Kucan, 1996; McKeown, Beck, & Sandora, 1996). It is, as Beck and McKeown explain, "an approach to text-based instruction that was designed to facilitate building understanding of text ideas" (Beck, et al., 1997). Beck and McKeown developed the procedures after several years of research on textbooks (Beck, McKeown, & Gromoll, 1989). They found that textbooks were often difficult for students to understand because they often assumed that students had more prior knowledge of the topics being dealt with than they actually did. As a result, the explanations of ideas and events given in the text were often insufficient to allow students to construct much meaning. This shortcoming of the textbooks was further compounded by the fact that students assumed the texts to be absolute authorities and thus beyond question. When students read a text and did not understand what they had read, they repeatedly saw themselves as totally responsible for their lack of understanding and failed to even consider the possibility that the text itself might be less than perfect.

Prompted by these findings, Beck and McKeown developed QtA with two ideas in mind: They wanted to encourage and assist young readers in getting under the surface of the material they were reading, dig into it, and engage with the ideas the texts presented. They also wanted to assist students in realizing that textbooks are simply someone's ideas written down and that readers frequently need to work hard to figure out what it is the author is trying to say.

Their procedure for doing this is simple and straightforward. First, the teacher explains to children that texts are in fact written by ordinary people who are not perfect and who create texts that are not perfect. Consequently, readers need to continually work hard to figure out what the authors are trying to say. Once students understand this reality, QtA proceeds by having the class read a text together, with the teacher stopping at critical points to pose queries that invite students to explore and grapple with the meaning of what is written. The queries include initiating prompts such as "What's the author trying to say?" to get students started in grappling with the text, follow-ups such as "What does the author mean by that?" to encourage them to dig for deeper meaning, and follow-ups such as "How does that connect with what the author told you" to encourage their putting ideas together. However, queries are not scripted, and teachers are encouraged to modify those suggested and make up their own queries to fit the students and texts they are working with.

Key attributes of Questioning the Author (QtA) are shown in Figure 1.

Figure 1. Key Attributes of Questioning the Author

The purpose of QtA is to assist students in building understanding from text.

Texts are prompts that constrain meaning but that frequently require the reader to interact and grapple with the information they provide.

QtA involves whole-class discussions in which the students and their teacher read and discuss relatively small segments of text.

QtA discussion occur "on line," that is, as students are engaged in their first reading of the text.

Queries are prompts that teachers use to assist students in engaging with the text, grappling with its meaning, and building understanding from it.

Queries foster discussion of the text and its meaning rather than wide-ranging discussion of matters only tangentially related to the text.

As the figure indicates and as we noted above, the key purpose of QtA is building understanding from text. As Beck and McKeown note, understanding does not come from a casual reading of the text and the assumption that the author's meaning will somehow be absorbed by the reader. Instead, understanding comes when the reader considers, manipulates, grapples with, and integrates information gleaned from the text with his existing knowledge. QtA involves students in a whole-class discussion that invites and prompts this sort of grappling and integrating, and it does so as students are reading the text for the first time rather than after they have read or during a second reading.

This is a very important characteristics of QtA and one that distinguishes it from many other questioning and discussion techniques. To repeat, QtA takes place during the reading of the text rather than afterwards. Moreover, QtA takes place during students' first reading of the text rather than in a re-reading. This is important because the goal of QtA is that students will actually have the experience of constructing meaning for text as they are reading, not that they will be told about what they might have experienced after the fact.

Another very important characteristic of QtA that distinguishes it from many other questioning and discussion techniques is that QtA discussions focus specifically on the text. QtA discussions are not wide-ranging conversations in which students are encouraged to engage in sharing a wide range of opinions and ideas. Instead, the discussion focuses on clarifying, collaboratively constructing meaning for, and ultimately understanding the ideas in the text they are reading. The QtA queries are strategically used by the teacher to direct the discussion to that end. They are general probes that have a very specific purpose—engaging students in grappling with and constructing meaning for the ideas in a text.

In the remainder of our discussion of QtA, we present a segment of a QtA session, consider queries in a bit more detail, explain the process of planning a QtA session, characterize the sorts of discussion you are trying to prompt with QtA, and suggest how you might introduce QtA into a class.

A Sample Questioning the Author Segment

The following In the Classroom scenario, taken from Beck et al. (1997), shows a fifth-grade social studies class studying Pennsylvania history. The class had been working with QtA for some time and is quite skilled in grappling with text ideas. The class is discussing a text segment about the presidency of James Buchanan, a Pennsylvania native. The text indicated that many people believed that Buchanan liked the South better than the North because he believed that it was a person's choice whether or not to have slaves. Here is their discussion.

Fifth Graders Questioning the Author

The teacher began the discussion of this segment of the text as follows:

Teacher: All right. This paragraph that Tracy just read is really full of important information. What has the author told us in this important paragraph?

Laura: Um, they um think that Buchanan liked the South better because they, he said that it is a person's choice if they want to have slaves or not, so they thought um that he liked the South better than the North.

Teacher: Okay. And what kind of problem then did this cause President Buchanan when they thought that he liked the South better? What kind of problem did that cause?

Next, Janet gave her interpretation of how Buchanan's position on slavery might have affected the voters in Pennsylvania.

Janet: Well, maybe um like less people would vote for him because like if he ran for President again, maybe less people would vote for him because like in Pennsylvania we were against slavery and we might have voted for him because he was in Pennsylvania, because he was from Pennsylvania. That may be why they voted for him, but now since we knew that he was for the South, we might not vote for him again.

At this point, the teacher summarized Janet's remarks.

Teacher: Okay, a little bit of knowledge, then, might change people's minds.

Then, another student acknowledged Janet's explanation and offered some of his own thoughts.

Jamie: I have something to add on to Janet's cause I completely agree with her, but I just want to add something on. Um, we might have voted for him because he was from Pennsylvania so we might have thought that since he was from Pennsylvania and Pennsylvania was an antislavery state, that he was also against slavery. But it turns out he wasn't.

Finally, a third student, acknowledged her classmates' thoughts and contributed her ideas to the developing interpretation.

Angelica: I agree with the rest of them, except for one that um, like all of a sudden, like someone who would be in Pennsylvania you want to vote for them but then they wouldn't, they be going for the South and then you wouldn't want to vote for them after that.

The scenario illustrates several key attributes of a QtA discussion. The students are indeed grappling with meaning; they are really trying to understand the author's meaning. The students are focused on the meaning of the text. The teacher adroitly directs the discussion, but she does not dominate it. She leaves plenty of room for student input because the purpose is for the students to understand the text; if they're the ones who are going to understand the text, they're the ones who must do most of the talking and thinking. The students respond at some length. Finally, they listen to each other and build on each others' responses as they jointly construct meaning for the text.

Queries

One way to begin to understand queries is to contrast them to traditional questions, something we are more familiar with. Beck and McKeown suggest three dimensions on which the two differ. First, traditional questions assess comprehension with the goal of finding out whether the students understood what they have read. Queries "assist students in grappling with text ideas" with the goal of helping them construct meaning. Second, traditional questions serve to evaluate individual student responses and foster teacher-to-student exchanges. Queries "facilitate group discussion about an author's ideas and prompt student-to-student interactions." Finally, traditional questions are generally used either before reading or after reading. Queries "are used on-line during initial reading" of the text.

As we have already pointed out, queries are not scripted and teachers are encouraged to adjust their queries to fit their students, the text, and the purposes in reading the text. Nevertheless, Beck and McKeown have identified a set of queries that are quite useful and that serve to illustrate the nature of successful queries. These are shown in Figure 2.

Figure 2. Some Questioning the Author Queries

Initiating Queries

What is the author trying to say here?

What is the author's message?

What is the author talking about?

Follow-Up Queries

So what does the author mean right here?

Did the author explain that clearly?

Does that make sense with what the author told us before?

How does that connect with what the author has told us here?

But does the author tell us why?

Why do you think the author tells us that now?

Narrative Queries

How do things look for this character now?

How does the author let you know that something has changed?

How has the author settled that?

Given what the author has already told us about this character, what do you think he (the character) is up to?

These, of course, are general queries. In posing queries for a specific text, they become more specific. We have already seen specific examples of initiating and follow-up queries in the QtA segment on President Buchanan. Here, the teacher's initiating query and its lead-in were "All right. This paragraph that Tracy just read is really full of important information. What has the author told us in this important paragraph?" In this same segment, one of the teacher's follow-up queries was "Okay. And what kind of problem then did this cause President Buchanan when they thought that he liked the South better? What kind of problem did that cause?"

Narrative queries, a type we haven't yet discussed, are uniquely suited to narratives. They are used with narratives in addition to initiating and follow-up queries. A representative example of a narrative query comes from a teacher whose class was using QtA as they read George Seldon's *The Cricket in Times Square* (1970). In the part of the story students have just read, Mario Bellinis's pet cricket Chester ate half of a two dollar bill. This is a problem because two dollars is a lot of money to the Bellinis. Here is the next paragraph of the story.

Chester Cricket sat frozen on the spot. He was caught red handed, holding the chewed-up two dollars in his front legs. Muttering with rage, Mama Bellinis picked him up by his antennae, tossed him into the cricket cage and clicked the gate behind him. He half expected that she would pick him up, cage and all, and throw him onto the shuttle tracks.

And here is the teacher's narrative query on it: "How do things look for Chester?"

As you can see from the sample queries and these examples, the purposes of initiating queries are to make the text information public in the classroom and to get the discussion underway, and the purposes of follow-up queries are to keep the discussion focused and to assist students in elaborating and integrating ideas. As you can also see, the purposes of narrative queries are to focus students' attention on characters and the roles they are playing in the story and on the way the author is crafting the plot.

Planning

There are three steps in planning a QtA lesson. The first step is to read and study the text thoroughly in order to identify the major understandings that you want students to achieve and the potential problems that they may have in achieving those understandings. For example, in reading the text on President Buchanan mentioned above, the teacher might determine that one thing she wants students to understand is that President Buchanan was supported and influenced by people representing diverse views and had to somehow deal with these diverse views. She might further infer that students were unlikely to appreciate the very different views on the matter or slavery advanced by different states.

The second step is to segment the text, to divide it into short sections that are read and discussed before students go on to the next section. Sometimes a segment will be quite lengthy, perhaps a page or so. At other times, a segment will be relatively short, for example, the sample discussion we presented for the Buchanan text dealt with a single paragraph—"All right. This paragraph that Tracy just read is really full of important information. What has the author told us in this important paragraph?" At still other times, a segment might be even shorter, dealing with a single sentence as fifth grade teacher Rona Greene tells us.

My fifth graders are familiar with the Questioning the Author procedure, so when I come up with just a single sentence for them to analyze, they're not surprised. Recently, while reading R. Lawson's *Ben and Me* (1939), I ran across a sentence that was challenging enough

166

and important enough to constitute a Questioning the Author segment. In the story, in which Benjamin Franklin has a mouse companion named Amos, who narrates the story, there comes a point at which Franklin is about to send Amos up in a kite to examine lightening. The text reads, "This question of the nature of lightening so preyed upon his mind that he was finally driven to an act of deceit that caused the first and only rift in our long friendship." I decided that this particular sentence, which indirectly reveals the depth of the friendship between Amos and Franklin but does not directly describe it, was worth serious consideration.

Rona Greene, Fifth Grade Teacher

Finally, in addition to deciding what is important in a text, what the likely stumbling blocks are, and how the text will be segmented for the discussion, you need to plan the actual queries to address to students. Although many queries will be modified or even discarded as the discussion proceeds, queries like "What has the author told us in this important paragraph?" and "How do things look for Chester?" are planned in advance.

Discussion

We have already given one fairly lengthy example of a QtA discussion and said several things about the sort of discussions that QtA is designed to foster. Here, we give another example of a QtA discussion, this too from Beck et al. (1997), and conclude with a quotation emphasizing that students need to be the principal participants in QtA discussions.

The discussion deals with the sentence from *Ben and Me* just given— "This question of the nature of lightening so preyed upon his mind that he was finally driven to an act of deceit that caused the first and only rift in our long friendship"—and begins with the initiating query shown in the dialog on the next page.

Questioning the Author Dialog

Teacher:	What's the author trying to tell us about Ben and Amos?
Temika:	That their friendship was breaking up.
Ms. Greene:	Their friendship was breaking up? OK, let's hang on to that. What do you think, April?
April:	I agree with the part that their friendship did break up, but um, I think that they got back together because when you were reading um, further, it said that he was enjoying the mouse.
Teacher:	OK, so let me make sure. You say that he knows that they're friends, and something happened that made them almost not be friends? But they're still friends?
Alvis:	I think that um, Amos is just, I think Amos is just lying because in the story it said if they weren't good friends, why would um, um, Ben build a um, kite for, build a kite for him so he could have fun.
Teacher:	OK, so Alvis is telling us that, why would Ben go to all that trouble and build that beautiful kite if they weren't friends? A lot of people agreed that their friendship was broken up. Alex doesn't think their friendship is broken up. Can somebody help me out? What's the author want us to figure out here?

(The teacher saw that April and Alvis were making sense of this sentence by bringing in supporting information from other parts of the text, and she attempted to rephrase their statements to better clarify the nature of the friendship.)

The discussion continues, with two more students grappling with the meaning of the sentence.

Tammy:	Um, um, deceit was an act of lying so that means, that means um, sometimes a lie broke up a friendship and, because it made a rift and um, so, and deceit was an act of lying, so their friendship must've broke up because of somebody told um, some kind of lie.
Teacher:	Oh, that's interesting. Tammy said that if there were some lying going on, something to break up their friendship, because that's what Amos said, "the

first and only rift in our friendship," something must've happened. How many of you agree that something had to happen?

Jamal: I disagree, cause a break in their friendship don't mean they gotta break their friendship.

Teacher: OK, so Jamal thinks that they might still be friends, even though something happened. OK? We're gonna continue 'cause the only way we're gonna find out is if we read some more.

In addition to illustrating how a teacher rephrases and clarifies ideas and keeps the discussion focused as she guides students toward full understanding of this important sentence, this excerpt shows how QtA discussions are dominated by students rather than by teachers: "Students do the work. They construct the meaning, wrestle with the ideas, and consider the ways information connects to construct meaning." Thus, "the discussion becomes an opportunity for students to formulate complete thoughts, respond to the text, react to each other's ideas, and consider new notions" (Beck et al., 1997).

Introducing QtA

Introducing QtA is a straightforward matter, but it is important to include several points in your introduction. First, tell students that the way they are going to be reading and discussing text is probably different from they way they have typically dealt with it. Next, tell them that what you and they are going to be doing is reading and discussing short sections of text at some length. That is, they will read a segment of text and then stop and discuss what it means with their classmates. After that, explain that the reason they need to do this is that a text is simply somebody else's words written down and that sometimes, in fact in quite a few cases, understanding what the author is saying requires close attention to and a good deal of discussion of the text. Finally, note that the discussions you are going to have will deal with the text and the meaning the author is trying to convey rather than with more wide ranging matters.

That's it. With this ground work laid, and of course after thoroughly familiarizing yourself with the QtA procedure, you are ready to begin QtA sessions.

Questioning the Author's Impact

Beck and McKeown and their colleagues have worked with QtA for several years, and have gathered several sorts of data on its efficacy. First, they implemented QtA with two teachers who showed the traditional pattern of teacher-initiated questions aimed mainly at retrieving information directly form the text and brief student responses that were quickly acknowledged before the next questions was asked.

But with QtA, their lessons began to change. Typically, a QtA lesson showed collaborative construction of meaning. A student would offer an idea in response to a query, and the teacher and other students would build on and elaborate that idea. As an example, here is a brief excerpt from a QtA social studies lesson on "international cooperation." The class had just read a text segment about countries cooperating to share resources through world trade.

Teacher: What's the author reminding us of here? Reggy?

Reggy: That we, um, that we trade countries out of their resources and they trade us out of our resources and we cooperate, by helping each other.

Notice in the above excerpt that Reggy's response is in own words, strongly suggesting that he is presenting his own ideas rather than simply parroting text information. Now notice in the following excerpt how the teacher handles Reggy's response by summarizing part of it and then extending the discussion by forming a question from another piece of what Reggy said.

Teacher: OK, Reggy said we help each other, and that's how we cooperate. When you cooperate, you're working together to get something done. What does Reggy mean by, "we trade resources out of their country?" What's he talking about? Darleen?

Darleen responds with an explanation about how trade works.

Darleen: He's talking about, when he says we're trading resources out of our country, he means that other countries, like Britain and Japan and China, we get our cotton and our resources that we have that are really popular, and we trade them for money sometimes.

Darleen's response is a fitting conclusion to our discussion of QtA because it indicates the amount of listening, thinking, and connecting that a QtA lesson can elicit. This is the sort of active engagement students need to demonstrate if they are to fully understand a text.

References

Beck, I. L., McKeown, M. G., & Gromoll, E. W. (1989). Learning from social studies text. *Cognition and Instruction, 6,* 99-158.

Beck, I. L., McKeown, M. G., Hamilton, R., & Kucan, L. (1997). *Questioning the author: An approach for enhancing student engagement with text.* Newark, DE: International Reading Association.

Beck, I. L., McKeown, M. G., Hamilton, R., & Kucan, L. (1998). Getting at the meaning: How to help students unpack difficult text. *American Educator, 22* (1 & 2), 66-71-85.

Beck, I. L., McKeown, M. G., Worthy, J., Sandora, C. A., & Kucan, L. (1996). A year-long classroom implementation to engage students with text. *Elementary School Journal, 96,* 385-214.

McKeown, M. G., Beck, I. L., & Sandora, C. A. (1996). Questioning the author: An approach to developing meaningful classroom discourse. In M. F. Graves, P. van den Broek, & B. M. Taylor (Eds.), *The first R: Every child's right to read* (pp. 97-119). New York: Teachers College Press.

Seldon, G. (1999). *The cricket in Times Square.* New York: Bantam.